Nelson Comprehension

Teacher's Resource Book

4

Wendy Wren
Donna Thomson
Doug Dickinson
Series Editor: John Jackman

Nelson Thornes

Published in 2009 by:
Nelson Thornes Ltd
Delta Place
27 Bath Road
CHELTENHAM
GL53 7TH
United Kingdom

09 10 11 12 13 / 10 9 8 7 6 5 4 3 2 1

A catalogue record for this book is available from the British Library

ISBN 978 1 4085 0508 3

Page make-up by Topics – The Creative Partnership, Exeter

Cover image illustration by Studio Pulsar at Beehive Illustration

Printed and bound in Croatia by Zrinski

Pupil Book Illustrations by: Paul Moran, Pete Smith, Studio Pulsar, Studio Bugs, Gary Joynes, Bob Moulder, Mark Draisey, Roger Penwill, Russ Daff, Tony Forbes, Melanie Sharp, Mike Phillips and David Russell Illustration.

Pupil Book photographs courtesy of: Alamy 10, 11, 14, 47, 49 (axe), 49 (crown), 50 (Countess of Salisbury), 62, 63; Getty Images 42, 43, 44, 45, 49 (gate), 60, 61; iStock 20, 21, 28, 46, 50 (Anne Boleyn); NASA 12, 13; National Library of Australia 40, 41.

Acknowledgements
The author and publisher are grateful to the following for permission to reproduce copyright material:

Andersen Press Ltd for material from Melvin Burgess, *The Earth Giant* (1995) pp. 13-15; Clare Bevan for her poem, 'Coral Reef'; Egmont Books for material from Michael Morpurgo, *Why the Whales Came* (1985) pp. 80-82; Express Newspapers for Penny Stretton, 'The Northern Lights Fantastic', Daily Express, 20.12.08; David Higham Associates on behalf of the author for material from Michael Morpurgo, *The Ghost of Grania O'Malley*, Egmont (1996) pp. 81-82; and Michael Morpurgo, *Kensuke's Kingdom*, Egmont (1999) pp. 42-46; Julie Holder for her poem, 'The Loner'; Patricia Leighton for her poem, 'Bullied'; Patrick Nobes for material from his edition of *Frankenstein*, Hutchinson Education (1984) pp. 17-19; The Random House Group Ltd for material from Joe Simpson, *Touching the Void*, Jonathan Cape (2004) pp.71-73; Rogers Coleridge & White Ltd on behalf of the author for Brian Patten, 'The River's Story' from *Thawing Frozen Frogs* by Brian Patten, Viking Children's Books (1990). Copyright © Brian Patten 1990; and Jane Serraillier on behalf of the Estate of the author for material from Ian Serraillier, *The Enchanted Island*, Oxford University Press (1964) pp. 111-113. Copyright © 1964 Estate of Ian Serraillier.

Every effort has been made to trace the copyright holders but if any have been inadvertently overlooked the publishers will be pleased to make the necessary arrangement at the first opportunity.

Contents

Section A   Introduction   4

Section B   How Nelson Comprehension works   6

Section C   Glossary of comprehension terms   12

Section D   Using Nelson Comprehension ICT   14

Doug Dickinson

Section E   Nelson Comprehension and Assessment for Learning   20

Donna Thomson

Section F   Nelson Comprehension unit by unit   24

Section G   Using the Picture Snapshot Assessment   98

Donna Thomson

Introduction

Reading comprehension has always been a key component in the curriculum of children of all ages, especially children of primary school age. For many years this was seen principally as a means of assessing the extent to which children were truly understanding and interpreting what they had learnt to read. However, more recently, the extent to which developing the skills of reading comprehension can help build all-important thinking skills has become apparent.

While the debate has long been ongoing as to whether spelling is best 'caught or taught', consideration of whether comprehension skills are 'caught or taught' has attracted little or no attention. It seems to have been accepted that if pupils are asked to answer questions on what they have read enough times, they eventually 'get it'. But do they?

Some pupils intuitively understand what they have read on several levels, but the majority of pupils need to be 'taught' these skills in a structured, progressive way. A pupil working individually, reading a passage and answering questions, should be the final, rather than the initial, stage of the process. Helping pupils reach this final stage successfully is the basis for **Nelson Comprehension.**

To read effectively it has been said that pupils should learn to 'read the lines, read between the lines and read beyond the lines'. In other words, they need to acquire a literal understanding of the content, without which they can hardly reach first base. All the class need to be helped and encouraged to achieve this goal. But beyond this, most children should be helped to develop the skills of deduction and inference, whether in understanding a story or in retrieving information in a non-fiction text, or evaluating or critically analysing what they have read.

We believe that comprehension skills are the essential building blocks of effective learning throughout the curriculum, not just within literacy. They are crucial learning tools in most, if not all, subjects. So, can we risk that children will just 'get it'? We think not!

Nelson Comprehension has therefore been given far more structure and didactic content than previous courses. Each 'unit' in Books 1 to 4 comprises three elements: material devised to support class teaching; followed by group work; and finally offering opportunities for essential individual pupil activity. Unlike other courses, Nelson Comprehension unashamedly teaches comprehension. But, mindful of different requirements within different schools and classes, or even between different children within the same class, the content has been structured to allow flexibility so that, at the extreme, all parts of each unit can be worked through by an individual or small group working together.

To maximise the teaching opportunities, the passages, poems and extracts have been selected to complement requirements of the range of reading required at the relevant stages of the child's development. So, the content is not only appropriate to developing the skills of reading comprehension, but is supportive of other reading and writing requirements.

Nelson Comprehension is also a fully blended series. As well as the exciting and engaging (and fully self-supporting) print resources, the series is complemented with a stunning

range of ground-breaking ICT resources in which multimedia (voiceovers, sound effects, film, animations) are used to support comprehension. Not only do these enhance further the teaching and reinforcement of key comprehension skills, they also underline the fact that comprehension skills are as vital as ever in an age of electronic information, such as e-mails, internet, blogs and text messaging.

How Nelson Comprehension works

Nelson Comprehension works by using a unique three-stage approach to comprehension: starting with teaching key comprehension skills; then moving into pupils' own group discussion and drama activities to reinforce their learning of the key skills; then the final stage where children are presented with a new extract and a set of questions designed to assess what they've learnt.

Planning with Nelson Comprehension

The series covers all six primary year groups (Years 1 to 6, or Scottish P2 to P7) and each year group is split into ten teaching units. These provide coverage of the genres and text types the children are likely to encounter in that particular year: fiction, non-fiction and poetry. Each unit in **Nelson Comprehension** is linked to a specific genre or text type. For example: Year 3 Unit 1 'Familiar places' concerns stories with familiar settings. Within the 'Familiar places' unit, the familiar settings supplied for the extract are home *(The Laughing Snowman)*, the street *(The House of Coloured Windows)* and a new home *(Uninvited Ghosts)*.

Each unit is given a clear main objective, which is identified in the Pupil Book, and full guidance is also given for the *Renewed National Literacy Framework* objectives, *National Curriculum assessment focuses* and the *Scottish Curriculum for Excellence objectives* (see pages 24–27). Further guidance for Wales and Northern Ireland can be found on pages 22–23.

It is not intended that a **Nelson Comprehension** unit forms the basis for a whole framework planning unit which may cover three or four weeks. The work here is very much aimed at the early immersion or analysis phases of a unit of work, in which teaching comprehension skills is of paramount importance, prior to the pupils' planning and composition of their own text in the genre. The extracts are carefully chosen to engage the pupils' interest and maximise teaching and learning opportunities within a class setting. The authors would also recommend the titles from which the extracts are taken for pupils' own reading, or to be used as whole texts for more in-depth study as being excellent examples of the particular genre.

Teach

Each unit is split into three sections: *Teach*, *Talk* and *Write*. All three sections are designed with flexibility in mind, and can be

Carefully selected text extract to support unit focus.

Clear and engaging illustration.

Panel prompts to fully support whole-class and group teaching.

used in a variety of ways to suit the teachers' needs – whether for use with the whole class, small groups or individually.

Nelson Comprehension
Pupil Book 4
Unit 2 *Teach*

The *Teach* section is designed to support whole-class teaching. It provides an illustrated extract and a selection of 'prompt' questions. The teacher and pupils investigate the text using the panel prompts to focus the discussion on the relevant comprehension points/strategies. The teacher then models the strategies required so pupils can understand what is being asked and where and how to answer.

Each *Teach* extract is supplied in the Pupil Book and in this Teacher's Resource Book, where it is fully supported with assessment and answer guidance, and finally as an interactive multi-modal whiteboard version. The whiteboard version of the extract comes complete with questions, set highlights, illustrations, voiceovers, sound effects and, in some cases, animations and video.

The 'questions' in *Teach* are bullet pointed rather than numbered and appear to the right of the text in a 'prompt panel'. The two-page spread has been designed not to look like a typical comprehension exercise but rather as a shared activity where teacher and pupils engage in a class discussion based on the panel prompts.

Carefully selected and illustrated text
extract to support group work.

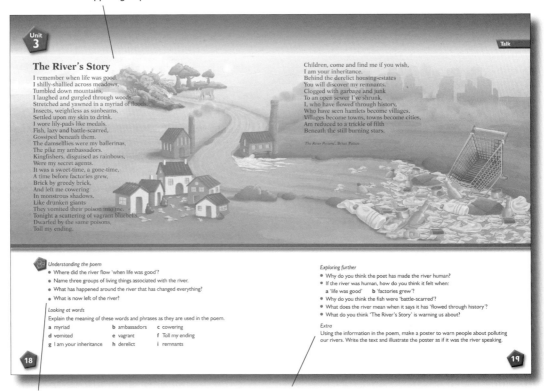

The River's Story

I remember when life was good.
I shilly-shallied across meadows,
Tumbled down mountains,
I laughed and gurgled through woods,
Stretched and yawned in a myriad of floods,
Insects, weightless as sunbeams,
Settled upon my skin to drink.
I wore lily-pads like medals.
Fish, lazy and battle-scarred,
Gossiped beneath them.
The damselflies were my ballerinas,
The pike my ambassadors.
Kingfishers, disguised as rainbows,
Were my secret agents.
It was a sweet-time, a gone-time,
A time before factories grew,
Brick by greedy brick,
And left me cowering
In monstrous shadows,
Like drunken giants
They vomited their poison into me.
Tonight a scattering of vagrant bluebells,
Dwarfed by the same poisons,
Toll my ending.

Children, come and find me if you wish,
I am your inheritance.
Behind the derelict housing-estates
You will discover my remnants.
Clogged with garbage and junk
To an open sewer I've shrunk,
I, who have flowed through history,
Who have seen hamlets become villages,
Villages become towns, towns become cities,
Am reduced to a trickle of filth
Beneath the still burning stars.

The River Poison', Brian Patten

Understanding the poem
● Where did the river flow 'when life was good'?
● Name three groups of living things associated with the river.
● What has happened around the river that has changed everything?
● What is now left of the river?

Looking at words
Explain the meaning of these words and phrases as they are used in the poem.

a myriad	b ambassadors	c cowering
d vomited	e vagrant	f Toll my ending
g I am your inheritance	h derelict	i remnants

Exploring further
● Why do you think the poet has made the river human?
● If the river was human, how do you think it felt when:
  a 'life was good'   b 'factories grew'?
● Why do you think the fish were 'battle-scarred'?
● What does the river mean when it says it has 'flowed through history'?
● What do you think 'The River's Story' is warning us about?

Extra
Using the information in the poem, make a poster to warn people about polluting
our rivers. Write the text and illustrate the poster as if it was the river speaking.

18

19

Questions arranged according to difficulty
in order to support differentiation.

Group presentation activity – usually
discussion, drama or composition activity.

Talk

Nelson Comprehension
Pupil Book 4
Unit 3 *Talk*

The *Talk* section is aimed at supporting group work and discussion
in order that pupils practise the comprehension strategies taught
in *Teach*. A new extract is provided, which the pupils can read
in turn, and then a series of questions are given for discussion,
starting with literal questions, and then moving on to questions
that require more complex comprehension skills, such as
inference and evaluation. The final 'Extra' activity is a discussion
or drama activity that usually requires the children to work
together to produce a performance, or debate a question or issue
from the extract, thereby allowing a widening of the scope of the
comprehension. This acts as a springboard into personal reflection
on what has been read. For example, 'Describe where you live.',
'What do you like about it?', 'What don't you like about it?'

As with *Teach*, each *Talk* extract is supplied in the Pupil Book,
Teacher's Resource Book (which supplies full assessment and
answer guidance) and for the whiteboard. The whiteboard extract
is supported by illustrations and two special 'Talk' activities –
interactive activities designed for groups to support the
'Extra' activity.

New illustrated text extract to support individual oral or written comprehension exercise.

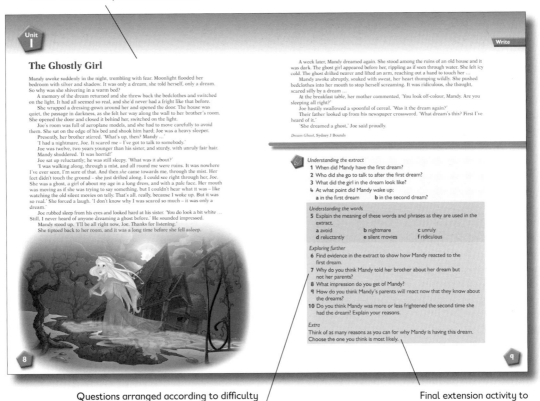

Questions arranged according to difficulty and colour-coded to support differentiation.

Final extension activity to round off the unit's work.

Write

Nelson Comprehension
Pupil Book 4
Unit 1 *Write*

The *Write* section is aimed at providing individual pupils with the chance to complete a set of comprehension questions so they can be assessed on the strategies they have been taught in *Teach* and *Talk*. While the questions can obviously be used for a full written test, they are also equally ideal for an oral question and answer/discussion activity. The questions are laid out in headed sections with colour banding in order to reflect four different sections (these equate essentially to literal, vocabulary, inference/evaluative and 'Extra') should the teacher wish to set only a part of the whole list of questions, to provide a differentiated task or to fit the time available. Full guidance for assessing the children's responses to the questions is in this Teacher's Resource Book.

An assessment sheet is also provided in this Teacher's Resource Book for each unit's *Write* section, which includes details on the specific question type and National Curriculum assessment focuses used. The assessment sheet (see example overleaf, and pages 88–97) can be used to fully support Assessment for Learning or the Assessing Pupil Progress initiative.

As with *Talk*, an 'Extra' activity is given in *Write*. This is usually a longer written or discussion activity that allows for a widening of the scope of the comprehension, and is a way to reflect and reinforce what has been learnt in the unit. For example:

Imagine you are Marion or Simon. You are in bed when the ghost comes out of the drawer. Write about:

- what you say
- what you do
- how you feel.

Hence, the key pattern for **Nelson Comprehension** is as follows:

- *Teach:* Pupils are taught in a whole class situation.
- *Talk:* Pupils practise with group support.
- *Write:* Pupils do comprehension individually.

Questions and differentiation

The 'prompts' or questions cover lower- and higher-order reading skills. Pupils in all three sections are asked to respond to three basic tiers of questions:

- *A **literal level***, for example, 'What was Mandy going to do if it snowed?'

- *An **inferential level***, for example, 'How do you know that Emma was the only one excited about the snow?'

- *A **personal/evaluative level***, for example, 'How do you feel about snow?'

These three core comprehension skills form the basis of further comprehension skills tested in this series: literal understanding enables information finding and summarising; inference enables interpretation and prediction; evaluation enables criticism, empathy and relating the child's own experience to a particular question or dilemma.

In addition, there is also a vocabulary section to encourage pupils to investigate and clarify the meanings of unknown words in context, using a dictionary if necessary. This strategy unlocks not only the meaning of the word but can have wider implications for the extract as a whole.

The questions in each section are therefore ordered carefully to relate to the ability level of the children, and can be easily broken up into differentiated 'blocks' to fit the needs of a particular ability group.

Introducing and rounding up

The unit notes in the Teacher's Resource Book include suggestions for a 'Before reading' discussion in order to elicit pupils' prior knowledge, thoughts and feelings about an important aspect of the extract or text they are about to read.

Then, after each extract, there is a plenary session (and at the end of each unit, a 'round-up'), which is closely based on class, group or individual work and allows for the reinforcement of comprehension skills and for the unit's key objective.

Picture Snapshot Assessment

A unique further feature of **Nelson Comprehension** is Picture Snapshot Assessment: a ground-breaking method of assessing a pupil's comprehension skills using ICT-based images and animation. This technique is particularly effective with children who are struggling readers, or whose comprehension skills may be masked by problems decoding text. For full details, see pages 98–111).

Glossary of comprehension terms

There are many comprehension terms that relate to the key comprehension strategies. The following are definitions of these terms and are also accompanied by an example of how they might be used as a comprehension question or statement.

Analysis
Identifying and commenting on the organisation, style or features of a text. Understanding the relationship between context, meaning and wording.

The playscript includes a <u>cast list</u>, <u>scene description</u>, <u>character parts</u> and <u>stage directions</u>.

Deduction
Judgement made from <u>inferred clues</u> to form a <u>conclusion</u>.

He realised the <u>show was over</u> when he walked in because he <u>heard applause</u> and <u>saw the actors bowing</u>.

Evaluation – *Personal meaning, empathy, response, opinion*
Looking at 'the bigger picture' – what you think from your own experience that explains the actions, feelings and motives of characters and links to information and mood within a narrative. Expressing and justifying an opinion based on information given.

I think the boy was <u>uneasy</u> about dancing <u>with Emily</u> because he <u>grimaced</u> and <u>stood</u> as <u>far away</u> from her as possible. I say that because the <u>teacher told him</u> to dance with her and Tom <u>didn't like being told</u> what to do. He was also probably <u>embarrassed</u> that the <u>other boys</u> were watching him.

Inference – *Implied and hidden meaning*
Thinking and searching for clues – providing evidence for deductions in answer to questions that ask '*How do you know that*' or '*Why?*' Information that is implied within the text but not given directly, from which connecting evidence is drawn to support deductions.

Q: Can the dragon breathe fire? How do you know?
A: <u>Yes, the dragon can breathe fire because smoke is coming from his nostrils</u> and <u>he has burned the trees next to his lair</u>.

Literal – *Explicit meaning*
Information is obvious and needs no interpretation (Who? What? Where? Right there!). The information is given directly on the page without need for inferring or evaluating to deduce an answer.

Q: <u>What colour</u> is the dragon?
A: The dragon is a <u>bright shade of green</u>.

Clarification – *Making sense of; making meaning clear*

Defining a word, phrase or concept as it is used in the text. Using appropriate language that accurately and meaningfully describes scenes, events, moods, actions and feelings expressed in a story or non-fiction text when retelling in own words.

Q: 'Use <u>appropriate language</u> that <u>accurately and meaningfully</u> describes scenes and events.' Explain what is meant by 'appropriate language' here.
A: I think 'appropriate language' here means <u>choosing words carefully</u> to <u>convey the same meaning</u> that was used in the text to describe the scenes and events.

Prediction

Anticipating cause and effect from implied, hidden and personal meaning within the text. Giving evidence-based reasons for what you think might have happened before, might be happening now or what might happen next to characters and events in a story.

Q: What will happen next?
A: I think the man <u>walking under the ladder</u> will get <u>covered in paint</u> because the worker <u>above him</u> has just <u>tipped over a tin of paint</u>.

Prior knowledge and experience

Personal history-based understanding, use of what you have already learned or experienced in your own life to predict or explain the meaning of something.

Q: It was a <u>hot spring day</u> on the <u>Cornish coast</u>. Why do you think the boy <u>preferred to stay out of the sea</u> and make sandcastles even though he thought the water <u>looked inviting</u>?
A: I think the boy preferred to stay out of the sea on a hot spring day even though he thought the water looked inviting because he knew that the <u>sea was usually too cold</u> for swimming during <u>springtime in Cornwall</u>.

Summarising / retelling

Gathering, organising and presenting key points of a story or non-fiction information in the correct sequence. Using the basic story structure of beginning, middle and end, a summary or retelling involves a person, action, place, problem and resolution.

The story is about a <u>boy</u> who is <u>playing on a beach</u> in <u>Cornwall</u> on a spring day. <u>He</u> wants to <u>go swimming in the sea</u> but the <u>water is too cold</u> so <u>he makes sandcastles instead</u>.

Using Nelson Comprehension ICT
Doug Dickinson

Doug Dickinson has worked in primary education for over 40 years, and is currently a lecturer at Leicester University and a primary ICT consultant for a number of primary ICT publishers, having worked for the National Literacy Strategy and Becta.

ICT and comprehension

Since Caxton, ordinary people have been decoding and trying to make sense of the printed word; they have brought their own interpretation to authors' texts and this has led, at times, to some amusing and some disastrous incidents. Today's texts look and feel different; they are not simply composed of words on a page but often come with drawings, photographs and diagrams all interlaced together to form a comprehensive whole.

As we move further into the 21st century, the power of electronic communication in all of our lives becomes more and more evident. Today, many developed texts written to be read for information and for pleasure are multimodal, arriving with the reader in an electronic format that contains all of the printable aspects of the past but also allows for sound, video and animation on pages that can be interrogated, zoomed, hyperlinked. This is a media-rich age, and it is the understanding, the putting into perspective and the dealing with the inferences of the texts presented that is the current life skill of comprehension.

It is the comprehension (the understanding) of all of these types of text that is the function of this exciting software package, which comes complete with age-grouped examples to help readers get the best out of the fiction and non-fiction that influences and excites their learning and recreation.

Teach

The aim of the *Teach* section is to provide a teacher with fully interactive whiteboard support for the teaching of key comprehension skills.

Each *Teach* section contains an illustrated extract, which comes with click-on highlights and question boxes. Each highlight either specifically answers the particular question or, in the case of an inference question, provides clues before offering possible answers/free type for the teacher (thereby offering a three-stage process: question – clues – possible answers; this is vital for teaching children inference, deduction and 'reading between the lines').

Teachers can also make their own annotations on the extract by using their own interactive whiteboard tools or the tools provided.

The readers engage with the quality text, perhaps in a whole class or group setting, or as a guided read displayed on an interactive whiteboard. Using the annotation tools (which dock to the left of the text, but which can also be moved to any position on the screen), the text can be explained and key points emphasised.

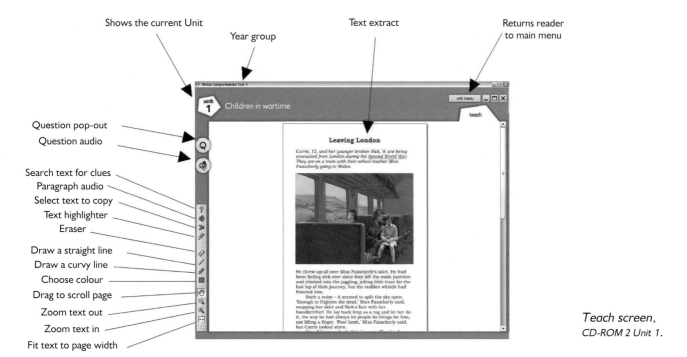

Shows the current Unit

Year group

Text extract

Returns reader to main menu

Question pop-out
Question audio

Search text for clues
Paragraph audio
Select text to copy
Text highlighter
Eraser
Draw a straight line
Draw a curvy line
Choose colour
Drag to scroll page
Zoom text out
Zoom text in
Fit text to page width

Teach screen,
CD-ROM 2 Unit 1.

The questions for comprehension are accessed by clicking the 'Question pop-out'. Each question is intended to guide a reader towards understanding of the text by requiring one of a range of comprehension skills, such as literal understanding, inference, deduction or evaluation. Clues within the text can be accessed (and become highlighted in the text) by clicking on the 'Show clue' button.

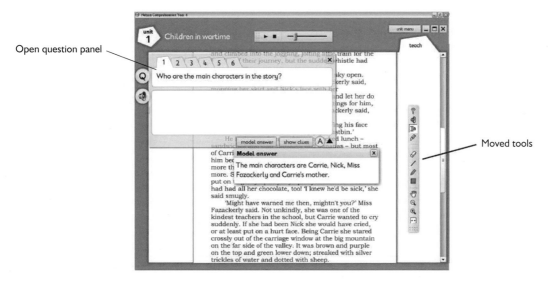

Open question panel

Moved tools

Answers to the questions can be inputted into the answer panel by clicking on the 'A' button. This opens a free writing panel. It is possible to copy and paste from the text into this panel if this is appropriate. A model answer is available for each question by clicking on the 'Model answer' button. This is intended as a guide and isn't necessarily the only answer – certainly, evaluation questions may well induce very different but equally plausible answers.

This *Teach* page has the capacity to utilise many multimedia functions to further learning and enrich comprehension (or to provide visual and audio to support a struggling reader). For example, the picture or the words can be toggled on or off (using the button in the bottom right of the picture or in the top left for the words), the sound can be switched on or off, and various other electronic supports, by way of video and animation, can all assist in the comprehension of the whole text. This multimedia provision facilitates different 'layers' of meaning – so, by adding or taking away images, voiceover or sound effects, a passage can be made easier, more difficult, or more accessible to children with different learning styles or to struggling readers with strong thinking skills.

Talk

The aim of the Talk section is to provide activities for children to work on in small groups – providing a stimulus for speaking and listening, drama and discussion – in order to reinforce important comprehension skills.

This section offers a new illustrated text extract and breakout activities for pairs and small groups of children to engage in supported and motivating discussion/role play/drama scenarios, based on a static extract screen (which may have illustrations). This is clearly a 'speaking and listening' activity.

The different activities can be amended (with imported assets or typed over script) in order to make work more or less challenging, or perhaps to fit a different piece of text.

Character / object grid (including thesaurus)

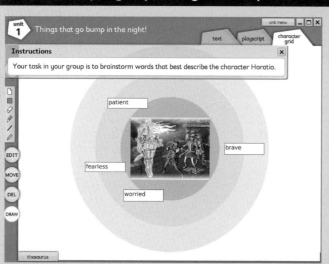

The 'Character grid' gives an opportunity for a group or class to develop vocabulary to describe characters in the text and place them within zones of relevance. By doing so, it stimulates the children to explore key characters, to empathise with their situation, to evaluate their character within the story, as well as to extend their descriptive vocabulary. The grid is also used with story settings and objects of inherent importance to the texts.

The top four buttons on the default toolbar allow users to move between edit, move and interact, delete, and draw and annotate functions. Each function has its separate set of extra tools to add exciting, personalised dimensions to the activity.

The excellent 'Media bank' is accessed from the 'edit' toolbar .

Another feature available from the 'Media bank' which allows for creativity in this section is the 'avatar maker'. Accessing this allows users to create and mould their own characters to be represented in the 'Character grid'.

The 'Character grid' also has a 'thesaurus' tool, which supports users in selecting appropriate words for the zones. Words from the thesaurus can be copied and pasted into a zone or it can be searched for suitable synonyms, thus extending user vocabulary.

The main text for the activity can always be accessed for reference by clicking on the text tab.

Story map

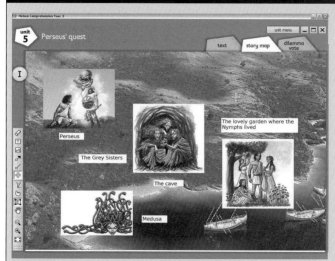

The 'Story map' uses similar functionality to the 'Character grid'. It allows users to review the text, identifying key events in sequence, and confirm their understanding by annotating the adjustable text blocks. It can also be used like a diagram with label and caption boxes.

Question maker

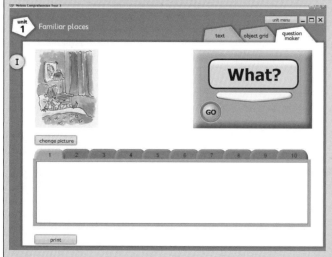

The 'Question maker' allows users to generate questions about characters and situations. The 'questioners' use the 'I' button on the screen to get instructions about the activity, together with the 'question generator' (which provides the 'Who?', 'What?', 'How?', 'Why?', 'When?' and 'Where?' question starters). They type their questions into the answer boxes (clicking on the tabs in turn) and then the character, in role, provides the answers. The skill of creating the right questions to find the information or answers they wish to know is of immense importance in developing key comprehension skills.

Each unit that utilises the 'Question maker' has its own set of instructions providing range and depth of activity.

Dilemma vote

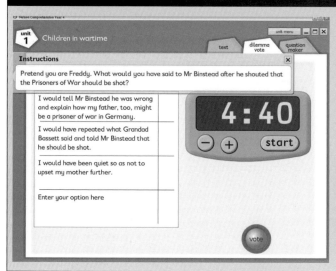

The readers are presented with a dilemma from a new text which they discuss and then vote on several options. There is a 'free type' option to give the group the opportunity to develop their own ideas. The dilemma could involve prediction, or evaluating and giving an opinion, or using inference to deduce an answer.

The default time for discussion is set to five minutes but this can be altered to suit the local situation.

In a class situation, the groups decide if they want to add another option and, once this has been agreed, start the timer and discuss the dilemma. Ideally, some of these discussions could be digitally recorded so that the quality of the discussion could be reviewed and each person's part in it evaluated. This would also support the collection of evidence of speaking and listening for APP (Assessing Pupil Progress).

When the discussion time is ended the individuals in the group then vote on their personal choice of solution to the dilemma. The idea is that they vote based on the arguments they have heard in the discussion time. To vote they simply click on the 'vote' button and the 'ballot box' will appear. They then place their 'X' next to their choice of solution and click the 'ballot box' again. An animation will show that their vote has been cast! To see how the votes add up simply click on the 'chart' button.

Info categoriser / Sequencer

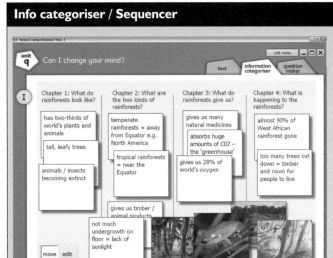

Info categoriser

This amazingly powerful application allows users to organise their knowledge gained from their understanding of the text. Each of the prepared facts or images can be edited and placed into the frameworks provided. The boxes can be edited, so the 'Info categoriser' can actually be used as a planning or research tool for further written work. As a tool it is ideal as a means to test a pupil's ability to analyse and organise information.

Clicking on the 'I' button gives instructions for the activity.

Sequencer

The 'Sequencer' allows users to do exactly what it says – sequence events or ideas in words or pictures. It can be effectively used as a full-scale writing planner. Each of the items already added to the sequence can be edited and moved by accessing the buttons on the bottom right of the screen and extra items can be added into the blanks provided. Like the 'Info categoriser', the edit feature takes the activity beyond sequencing, allowing its use as a text planning tool, or as a way to retell or summarise a text extract. Clicking on the 'I' button gives instructions for each unit activity.

Media bank

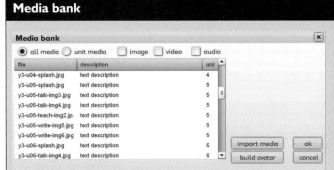

By clicking on the 'change picture' button (in the 'Question maker') or on the 'Media bank' icon (on the 'Character grid') a media bank is accessed, which allows for a variety of media types to be displayed in the 'Question maker' window. It is possible here to access all media from all installed units, or just the media for the displayed unit. Buttons on the bottom right of the 'Media bank' allow for personal media to be imported, such as an image or a film.

Text formatter

Make a playscript, Write a letter, Write insructions, Make an advert, Make an explanation, Make a poster

The 'Text formatter' allows users to create text-based contexts where the focus is on the quality of the literacy expressed through an understanding of the genre and the context of the unit. In the case of 'Make a playscript' the options allow a child to do just that, by providing playscript blocks on demand (for example, cast lists, scene descriptions and dialogue) so the child can focus on creating the content – whether it's transforming a prose passage into a playscript or creating another scene of the playscript.

The other text formatters work in a similar way and also allow the importation, through the 'Media bank', of images for illustration, which are particularly important in the case of 'Make an advert' or 'Make a poster'. The 'Text formatter' is ideal to support a child in understanding and analysing the organisation and structure of different text types.

Talk activity	Comprehension skills	Related AFs
Dilemma vote	prediction; inference; evaluation – opinion, empathy; historical/cultural context	AF2, AF3, AF6, AF7
Character/object grid	analysis – language use; evaluation – opinion, empathy; historical/ cultural context	AF5, AF7
Question maker	literal; inference; evaluation	AF2, AF3, AF6
Info categoriser	inference; analysis – text structure	AF3, AF4
Sequencer	summarising; analysis – text structure	AF2, AF4
Story	map visualisation; summarising; analysis – text structure	AF2, AF4
Text formatter	analysis – text structure/language use; inference; prediction; evaluation	AF3, AF4, AF5, AF6

Write

The aim of this section is to provide a means of reviewing the Pupil Book Write activities as a class/group in order to reinforce and build on the skills taught and learnt in the unit as a whole. This section is provided with a separate, but complementary, illustrated text (which can also be used as a teaching tool if teachers prefer) with around 10 questions of different types. The focus here, as in Teach, is on the use of the extract–questions–clues–blank–model answer sequence as a way of reviewing the children's written or even oral answers.

The tools available are complementary to those available in the Teach section of each unit, so as well as the 10 set questions (with highlights and clues) there is the option for the teacher or a pupil to make their own annotations and highlights on the text extract.

Picture Snapshot Assessment

The 'Picture Snapshot Assessment' is an exclusively electronic means of assessing a struggling reader's comprehension and thinking skills using visual images or animations (often accompanied by audio effects) as a basis for questions. This section is also supplied with an assessment tool that can be used as a basis for future planning for an individual pupil's needs.

The assessments here are based on users showing their ability to comprehend and answer questions that demonstrate literal, evaluation, inference, prediction and classification understanding. A simple summary is available of the results to sit alongside the evidence gathered for APP. For full details of the 'Picture Snapshot Assessment', see pages 98–111 of this book.

Nelson Comprehension and Assessment for Learning
Donna Thomson

Comprehension is a fundamental component of reading. Children need to understand that alongside 'accurate decoding of text', 'reading involves making meaning from content, structure and language' (QCA, 2006). However, children do not learn these skills without instruction. To become fluent readers they must not only be taught how to decode words accurately but also learn how to understand and interpret the author's meaning.

Assessing Pupil Progress

Comprehension assessment provides teachers with a wealth of information and is central to effective teaching and learning. The primary purpose for asking readers a range of comprehension questions is to find out what they need to be taught to support their understanding of text. Comprehension assessment offers teachers an insight into a reader's depth of thinking during and after reading. It tells them whether they are making sense of incoming information; whether they are able to infer, evaluate and justify responses to questions about the text; and how much they understand and are able to personally relate to the author's meaning.

The assessment focus (AF) criteria used to help teachers to assess pupil's reading progress clearly reflect the importance of comprehension in the development of good reading skills. Six out of the seven National Strategy assessment focuses refer to comprehension competencies and are directly linked to the criterion of National Curriculum levels (see the National Strategy grid).

Assessing Pupil Progress (APP) provides teachers with an effective structure for tracking children's learning and helps them to tailor their teaching to meet the needs of developing readers. It helps teachers to identify weaknesses and strengths through day-to-day and periodic assessment in relation to specific assessment focuses, and enables them to monitor the impact teaching and planning from AF evidence has on other areas of the pupils' learning. Intervention using these indicators raises standards of attainment in reading and across the curriculum, which in turn improves SATs results and ensures that children experience a smoother transition to secondary education.

Gathering assessment focus evidence for APP

Children's written responses to comprehension provide easy access to AF evidence. The Nelson Comprehension series provides a focus for this evidence using a range of quality extracts and carefully thought-out questions that support the teaching of the comprehension strategies.

However, in practice much of the evidence that is gathered in order to check a child's reading level and progression occurs in passing, through discussion and questioning about texts – particularly in Key Stage 1.

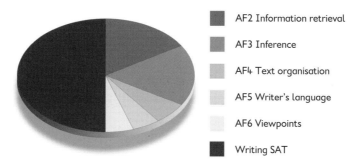

- AF2 Information retrieval
- AF3 Inference
- AF4 Text organisation
- AF5 Writer's language
- AF6 Viewpoints
- Writing SAT

2008 SATs
Marks break-down

The range of extracts and activities within the Nelson Comprehension series offer an excellent opportunity for discussion and oral responses to questions, particularly the *Teach* and *Talk* sections. Guided and shared reading offer valuable opportunities for teachers to explore a range of fiction and non-fiction through discussion and questions that help to develop and monitor children's understanding of text. Another activity that guides and develops comprehension is Reciprocal Reading (Palicsar and Brown, 1986), recommended by the Revised National Strategy, 2006. The 'Picture Snapshot Assessment' (see the CD-ROMs and pages 98–111 of this book) offers a means of building these skills.

Other speaking and listening activities that enable teachers to assess children's comprehension on a day-to-day basis are as follows:

- retelling from stories, a newspaper report or instructions, etc., where children are required to select the main ideas, sequence them correctly and say them coherently in their own words (AFs 2, 3, 4)

- drama, where children re-enact something they have read that relies on gathering and organising key information, interpretation and sequencing skills (AFs 2, 3, 4)

- 'hot-seating', where children act out characters from a story and others ask them questions that they need to answer in character role – in as much detail as possible – which draws on main and inferred ideas from story, interpretation of character and ideas, deduction and reference to text (AFs 2, 3, 4, 6).

There are examples of all these types of activity within the Nelson Comprehension series, and these are supported by the ICT Talk activities on the CD-ROM – such as the sequencer, the info categoriser, the dilemma vote and the question maker (for more details see 'Using Nelson Comprehension ICT' on pages 14–19).

Assessment focuses are also linked to different types of comprehension question and answer. For example, literal questions ask the children to locate the main 'who?', 'what?', 'where?' information from text to answer questions (AF2). Inference questions ask children to infer, deduce and provide evidence for their answers from text (AF3). Evaluation questions ask the children to empathise with characters using their own life experience and knowledge to explain the characters' behaviour or possible motives (AF6), and clarification questions ask about vocabulary and the author's use of language (AF3 and AF5).

Each unit comes with its own assessment grid, providing the 'Write' questions and activities along with guidance on question type, relevant assessment focus and a helpful marking system that can help inform your judgement on how well a child is using his/her comprehension skills. These can be found on pages 88–97 of this Teacher's Resource Book.

AF	AF description	Skills covered
AF2	Understand, describe, select or retrieve information, events or ideas from texts and use quotation and reference to text	literal, information finding, summarising
AF3	Deduce, infer or interpret information, events or ideas from texts	visualisation, inference, deducing information, prediction, clarification, drawing on prior knowledge
AF4	Identify and comment on the structure and organisation of texts, including grammatical and presentational features at text level	analysis of text structure
AF5	Explain and comment on writers' uses of language, including grammatical and literary features at word and sentence level	analysis of language use
AF6	Identify and comment on writers' purposes and viewpoints, and the overall effect of the text on the reader	evaluation – empathy, author viewpoint, opinion, criticism, previous experience
AF7	Relate texts to their social, cultural and historical contexts and literary traditions	evaluation – social, cultural, geographical and historical contexts

Full reading assessment guidelines are supplied on the DCSF Standards site.

Although reading and written comprehension is key to assessing children's depth of thinking, range of vocabulary and understanding of text, there are a number of children this does not suit because they struggle when decoding words on the page. They may have good inference skills, a rich verbal vocabulary and impressive understanding of the author's intention in discussion about text that has been read to them. However, these high-level skills are unlikely to be reflected in their responses to questions when they have had to read the text by themselves. As a result, they are likely to be assessed as 'poor' readers when it is actually their decoding that has failed at this level, rather than their 'whole' reading ability. It is important, therefore, that pupils can be assessed as much for their ability to infer, evaluate and comprehend the author's meaning, as they are for their decoding ability.

Nelson Comprehension's 'Snapshot Assessment' (see pages 98–111) offers an innovative solution to the problem of assessing the comprehension skills of struggling decoders. It also provides an effective comprehension measure for more able decoders who may already be assumed to be 'good readers' simply on the basis that they have fluent word recognition.

Using Nelson Comprehension with other curricula

Assessment for Learning and reading comprehension are at the heart of all the primary national curricula. As well as the English Primary National Literacy Strategy and Assessing Pupil Progress, the Scottish Curriculum for Excellence, the revised Northern Irish Curriculum for Key Stages 1 and 2, and the new

Welsh Key Stage 1 and 2 Curriculum all emphasise the need for the following key elements of assessment for learning:

- Sharing learning intentions with the children.

- Using day-to-day observation, along with discussion, oral activities and written activities, when assessing a child's comprehension skills.

- Adjusting teaching according to each child's assessment needs arising from these formative assessments.

Northern Ireland Key Stage 2 objectives	English Guidance for Key Stage 2 (Wales)
Talking and Listening Nelson Comprehension offers opportunities to engage with the following objectives: • Listening and responding to a range of fiction, poetry, drama and media texts. • Group and class discussions for a variety of purposes – responding to and evaluating ideas, arguments and points of view. • Telling, retelling and interpreting stories based on personal experiences and literature.	Nelson Comprehension supports the following lines of progression for: **Oracy** *Listening with understanding* (levels 1 to 5) – from paying attention to what is said to responding with questions and comments and more perceptive contributions. *Participation in discussion* (levels 1 to 6) – from taking part in a conversation to managing turn-taking and intervening, listening to others and taking account of discussion. *Expressing opinion* (levels 3 to 6) – from expressing opinion simply, developing response and justifying opinion offering evidence and with sensitivity to others.
Reading Nelson Comprehension offers opportunities to engage with the following objectives: • Reading and exploring a range of traditional and electronic texts, using drama, art and discussion to focus on distinctive features. • Representing stories and information texts in a range of visual forms and diagrams. • Justifying responses logically, by inference, deduction or reference to evidence within the text. • Discussing and considering aspects of stories, for example themes, characters, plots, places, objects and events. • Begin to be aware of how different media present information, ideas and events in different ways.	**Reading** *Reading increasingly demanding texts* (levels 1 to 5) – developing independent reading, using appropriate reading strategies and understanding texts of increasing length, complexity and sophistication. *Response to texts, including analysing and evaluating* (levels 1 to 6) – from simple likes and dislikes, to supporting preferences with reference to texts; identifying and responding to key features of texts, and critically appreciate texts. *Reading for information* (levels 1 to 6) – from locating information for a specific purpose, to collecting and synthesising for different purposes; developing appropriate reading strategies (skimming and scanning).
Writing Nelson Comprehension offers opportunities to engage with the following objectives: • Discuss various features of layout in texts which they are reading, so they can use them in their own writing.	

For links to the Renewed Primary Literacy Framework and the Scottish Curriculum for Excellence, please see individual unit descriptions.

Nelson Comprehension
unit by unit

Unit	Unit name	Skills	Genre/text type	Extracts	Renewed framework objectives
1	Things that go bump in the night!	Exploring atmosphere and tension	Ghost stories	*A Christmas Carol* Charles Dickens *Hamlet, Prince of Denmark* Ian Serraillier *Dream Ghost* Sydney J Bounds	**1** *Speaking* • Use talk to explore ideas, topics or issues. **3** *Group discussion and interaction* • Understand and use a variety of ways to criticise constructively and respond to criticism. **4** *Drama* • Devise a performance … **8** *Engaging with and responding to texts* • Compare how writers from different times and places present experiences and use language.
2	A life less ordinary	Understanding the structure of a biography	Biography	*Emmeline Pankhurst* *Neil Armstrong* *Louis Braille*	**1** *Speaking* • Use talk to explore ideas, topics or issues. **2** *Listening and responding* • Make notes … and discuss how note-taking varies depending on context and purpose. **3** *Understanding and interpreting texts* • Understand underlying themes, causes and points of view.
3	Painting a picture	Understanding themes and recognising personification	Poetry	*The Brook* Lord Tennyson *The River's Story* Brian Patten *Coral Reef* Clare Bevan	**1** *Speaking* • Use the techniques of dialogic talk to explore ideas, topics or issues. **3** *Group discussion and interaction* • Understand and use a variety of ways to criticise constructively and respond to criticism. **7** *Understanding and interpreting texts* • Understand underlying themes, causes and points of view.
4	Monstrous creations!	Creating characters and building tension	Fantasy and science fiction	*Frankenstein* Mary Shelley (adapted by Patrick Nobes) *The Earth Giant* Melvin Burgess *Jurassic Park* Michael Crichton (adapted by Gail Herman)	**1** *Speaking* • Use talk to explore ideas, topics or issues. **3** *Group discussion and interaction* • Understand and use a variety of ways to criticise and respond to criticism. **4** *Drama* • Devise a performance … **8** *Engaging with and responding to texts* • Compare how writers from different times and places present experiences and use language.
5	Which side are you on?	Understanding the conventions of argument	Argument	*Text messaging – good or bad?* *Animal testing* *UFOs do not exist!*	**1** *Speaking* • Use a range of oral techniques to present persuasive arguments and engaging narratives. **2** *Listening and responding* • Participate in whole class debate using the conventions and language of debate, including standard English. • Analyse and evaluate how speakers present points effectively … **7** *Understanding and interpreting texts* • Recognise rhetorical devices used to argue, persuade, mislead and sway the reader. **9** *Creating and shaping texts* • In non-narrative, establish, balance and maintain viewpoints.

Scottish C for E objectives	NC assessment focuses	Comprehension skills	ICT Talk activities
Listening and Talking *Understanding, analysing and evaluating (third / fourth levels)* Comments, with evidence, on the content and form of short and extended texts. **Reading** *Understanding, analysing and evaluating (third / fourth levels)* Identifies and discusses similarities and differences between different types of text.	AF3, AF7, *AF2, AF6*	**Literal** **Inference** **Clarification** ***Evaluation*** – empathy, opinion, prediction	Text formatter (playscript) Character grid
Listening and Talking *Finding and using information (third / fourth levels)* Makes notes and organises these to develop thinking, help retain and recall information, explore issues and create new texts, using own words. **Reading** *Finding and using information (second / third / fourth levels)* Using knowledge of features of text types, can find, select and sort information and use this for different purposes.	AF3, AF4, *AF2, AF6*	**Literal** **Summarising** **Inference** **Clarification** ***Evaluation*** – previous experience, opinion ***Analysis*** – text structure	Dilemma vote Question maker
Listening and Talking *Understanding, analysing, evaluating (third / fourth levels)* Shows understanding by giving detailed, evaluative comments, with evidence, about the content and form of short texts. **Reading** *Understanding, analysing, evaluating (third level)* Can comment, with evidence, on the content and form of short texts, and respond to literal, inferential and evaluative questions and other types of close reading tasks.	AF3, AF5, *AF2, AF6*	**Literal** **Inference** **Clarification** ***Analysis*** – language use ***Evaluation*** – opinion, author viewpoint	Text formatter (poster) Character grid
Listening and Talking *Understanding, analysing, evaluating (second / third levels)* Responds to literal, inferential, evaluative and other types of questions, asks different kinds of questions; comments with evidence on content and form of short texts. **Reading** *Understanding, analysing, evaluating (second / third levels)* Shows understanding across different areas of learning, identifies and considers the purpose and main ideas of a text and uses supporting detail; makes inferences from key statements.	AF3, AF5, *AF2, AF6*	**Literal** **Inference** **Clarification** ***Analysis*** – language use ***Evaluation*** – opinion, empathy	Question maker Character grid
Listening and Talking *Understanding, analysing, evaluating (second level)* Can distinguish fact from opinion and recognise influence. **Reading** *Finding and using information (second / third / fourth levels)* Using knowledge of features of text types, can find, select and sort information and use this for different purposes.	*AF2, AF6, AF3, AF5*	**Literal** **Inference** **Summarising** **Clarification** ***Analysis*** – text structure ***Evaluation*** – author viewpoint, criticism	Dilemma vote Information categoriser

Unit	Unit name	Skills	Genre/text type	Extracts	Renewed framework objectives
6	Finding a voice (poetry dealing with issues)	Exploring issues in poetry	Poetry	'The Loner' Julie Holder 'Bullied' Patricia Leighton 'The New Boy' John Walsh	**1** *Speaking* • Use a range of oral techniques to present persuasive arguments. • Participate in whole-class debate using the conventions and language of debate, including standard English. **3** *Group discussion and interaction* • Understand and use a variety of ways to criticise constructively and respond to criticism. **4** *Drama* • Improvise using a range of drama strategies and conventions to explore themes. **7** *Understanding and interpreting texts* • Understand underlying themes, causes and points of view.
7	Daring deeds	Explore how writers present experiences	Autobiography	*South* Sir Ernest Shackleton *20 HRS, 40 MIN… Our Flight in the Friendship* Amelia Earhart *Touching the Void* Joe Simpson	**1** *Speaking* • Use talk to explore ideas, topics or issues. **2** *Listening and responding* • Make notes and discuss how note-taking varies depending on context and purpose. **3** *Understanding and interpreting texts* • Understand underlying themes, causes and points of view. **8** *Engaging with and responding to texts* • Compare how writers from different times and places present experiences and use language.
8	The Tower of London	Understanding the conventions of formal writing	Formal writing	*The Tower of London* *A guide to the Tower of London* *Spectres of the Past*	**1** *Speaking* • Use talk to explore ideas, topics or issues. **2** *Listening and responding* • Identify the ways spoken language varies according to the differences in context and purpose. **7** *Understanding and interpreting text* • Understanding how writers use different structures to create coherence.
9	Danger at sea!	Understanding an author's themes and techniques	Authors and texts	*Why the Whales Came* Michael Morpurgo *The Ghost of Grania O'Malley* Michael Morpurgo *Kensuke's Kingdom* Michael Morpurgo	**1** *Speaking* • Use talk to explore ideas, topics or issues. **4** *Drama* • Improvise using a range of drama strategies and conventions to explore themes. **7** *Understanding and interpreting texts* • Understand underlying themes, causes and points of view.
10	Weird and wonderful	Understanding viewpoints in journalistic writing	Journalistic writing	*Devilish Doings in Devon* Henry Harris *Islands of Fire* *The Northern Lights Fantastic* Penny Stretton	**1** *Speaking* • Use a range of oral techniques to present persuasive arguments. • Use the technique of dialogic talk to explore ideas, topics or issues. **7** *Understanding and interpreting texts* • Understand how writers use different structures to create coherence and impact.

Scottish C for E objectives	NC assessment focuses	Comprehension skills	ICT Talk activities
Listening and Talking *Understanding, analysing, evaluating (third / fourth levels)* Shows understanding of the techniques of influence and persuasion. **Reading** *Understanding, analysing, evaluating (third level)* Can identify the purpose and main concerns of a text, infer meaning, and identify and discuss similarities and differences between different texts.	AF6, AF2, AF3, AF5, AF6	*Literal* *Inference* *Clarification* *Analysis* – language use *Evaluation* – empathy	Dilemma vote Character grid
Listening and Talking *Understanding, analysing, evaluating (second level)* Can recognise the difference between fact and opinion. **Reading** *Finding and using information (second / third / fourth levels)* Using knowledge of features of text types, can find, select and sort information and use this for different purposes.	AF3, AF6, AF2	*Literal* *Clarification* *Evaluation* – author viewpoint, empathy, opinion	Question maker Character grid
Listening and Talking *Understanding, analysing, evaluating (second level)* Can recognise the difference between fact and opinion. **Reading** *Finding and using information (second / third / fourth levels)* Using knowledge of features of text types, can find, select and sort information and use this for different purposes.	AF3, AF5, AF2, AF6, AF7	*Literal* – finding information *Inference* – deducing information *Clarification* *Analysis* – language use *Evaluation* – prior knowledge, author viewpoint	Story map Question maker
Listening and Talking *Understanding, analysing, evaluating (second / third levels)* Responds to literal, inferential, evaluative and other types of questions, asks different kinds of questions; comments with evidence on content and form of short texts. **Reading** *Understanding, analysing, evaluating (second / third levels)* Shows understanding across different areas of learning, identifies and considers the purpose and main ideas of a text and uses supporting detail; makes inferences from key statements.	AF3, AF5, AF2, AF6	*Literal* *Inference* *Clarification* *Evaluation* – previous experience, empathy, prediction	Dilemma vote Character grid
Listening and Talking *Understanding, analysing, evaluating (second level)* Can distinguish fact from opinion and recognise influence. **Reading** *Finding and using information (second / third / fourth levels)* Using knowledge of features of text types, can find, select and sort information and use this for different purposes.	AF2, AF4, AF3, AF6	*Literal* *Inference* *Clarification* *Evaluation* – opinion	Text formatter (article) Information categoriser

Things that go bump in the night!

▶ Exploring atmosphere and tension

Marley's Ghost

The cellar-door flew open with a booming sound, and then he heard the noise much louder, on the floors below; then coming up the stairs, then coming straight towards his door.

'It's humbug, still!' said Scrooge. 'I won't believe it.'

His colour changed though when, without a pause, it came on through the heavy door, and passed into the room before his eyes. Upon coming in, the dying flame leaped up, as though it cried, 'I know him! Marley's ghost!' and fell again.

The same face: the very same. Marley in his pigtail, usual waistcoat, tights, and boots ... The chain he drew was clasped about his middle. It was long and wound about him like a tail. It was made of cash-boxes, keys, padlocks, **ledgers**, deeds and heavy purses wrought in steel. His body was transparent, so that Scrooge observing him, and looking through his waistcoat, could see the two buttons on his coat behind ...

Nor did he believe it even now. Though he looked the **phantom** through and through, and saw it standing before him. Though he felt the chilling influence of his death-cold eyes ... he was still **incredulous**, and fought against his senses.

'How now!' said Scrooge, **caustic** and cold as ever. 'What do you want with me?'

'Much!' – Marley's voice, no doubt about it.

'Who are you?'

'Ask me who I *was*.'

'Who *were* you then?' said Scrooge, raising his voice ...

'In life I was your partner, Jacob Marley ... You don't believe in me,' observed the Ghost.

'I don't,' said Scrooge ...

At this the spirit raised a frightful cry, and shook its chain with such a dismal and appalling noise, that Scrooge held on tight to his chair to save himself from falling in a **swoon**. But how much greater was his

horror when, the phantom, taking off the bandage round his head as if it were too warm to wear indoors, its lower jaw dropped down upon its breast.

Scrooge fell upon his knees and clasped his hands before his face.

'Mercy!' he said. 'Dreadful **apparition**, why do you trouble me?'

'Man of the worldly mind!' replied the Ghost, 'do you believe in me or not?'

'I do,' said Scrooge. 'I must. But why do spirits walk the earth, and why do they come to me?'

'It is required of every man,' the Ghost returned, 'that the spirit within him should walk abroad among his fellow-men, and travel far and wide, and if that spirit goes not forth in life, it is condemned to do so after death. It is doomed to wander through the world – oh, woe is me – and witness what it cannot share, but might have shared on earth, and turned to happiness!' ...

'But you were always a good man of business, Jacob,' faltered Scrooge ...

'Business!' cried the Ghost, wringing his hands. 'Mankind was my business; the common welfare was my business; charity, mercy, **forbearance** ... Hear me! My time is nearly gone.'

'I will,' said Scrooge, 'but don't be hard on me!' ...

'I am here tonight to warn you, that you have yet a chance and hope of escaping my fate ... You will be haunted by Three Spirits.'

'Is that that chance and hope you mentioned, Jacob?' Scrooge demanded in a faltering voice.

'It is.'

'I – I think I'd rather not,' said Scrooge.

'Without their visits,' said the Ghost, 'you cannot hope to **shun** the path I tread. Expect the first tomorrow, when the bell tolls one.'

A Christmas Carol, Charles Dickens

- What is the name of the Ghost?
- Who is he haunting?
- Why did the Ghost make 'a frightful cry' and shake his chain?
- What did the Ghost tell Scrooge to expect tomorrow?
- Explain the meaning of the words in **bold**.
- How does Scrooge feel about the Ghost:
  - when it first appears
  - at the end of the extract?
- Why do you think the Ghost has to drag the chain around with him?
- What do you think the Ghost means when he says, 'It is required of every man, that the spirit within him should walk abroad among his fellowmen'?
- What do you think Scrooge means when he says that Jacob was 'a good man of business'?
- In your own words, explain why you think Scrooge is being haunted.

Extracts

A Christmas Carol Charles Dickens
Hamlet, Prince of Denmark Ian Serraillier
Dream Ghost Sydney J Bounds

Planning

Fiction genres – ghost stories

Objectives

Renewed Primary Literacy Framework Year 6
1 Speaking
• Use talk to explore ideas, topics or issues.
3 Group discussion and interaction
• Understand and use a variety of ways to criticise constructively and respond to criticism.
8 Engaging with and responding to texts
• Compare how writers from different times and places present experiences and use language.

Assessment focuses
AF3 Deduce, infer or interpret information, events or ideas from texts
L3–L4 Increasingly makes inferences based on evidence from different points in the text.
L5 Explains inferred meanings by drawing on evidence across the text.
AF7 Relate texts to their social, cultural and historical contexts and literary traditions
L4 Comments on features common to different texts, e.g. characters, settings, presentational features.
L5 Identifies and explains similarities and differences between texts, e.g. narrative conventions in ghost stories.

Scottish Curriculum for Excellence: Literacy
Listening and Talking
Understanding, analysing, evaluating (third / fourth levels)
Comments, with evidence, on the content and form of short and extended texts.
Reading
Understanding, analysing, evaluating (third / fourth levels)
Identifies and discusses similarities and differences between different types of text.

TEACH

In this unit pupils are given the opportunity to investigate ghost stories, which is a popular genre for this age group. The three extracts highlight the typical night scene of a 'visitation' and explicitly state or hint at the common feature that ghosts haunt for a reason! This unit and Unit 4 give pupils the opportunity to explore the features of two genres.

Before reading

• Do the pupils believe in ghosts?
• What ghost stories have they read or seen on television or DVD?
• Do they like ghost stories? Why? Why not?
• Discuss why and when ghosts haunt.

Reading

• Explain to pupils that they are going to read an extract from *A Christmas Carol*. The story so far: Ebenezer Scrooge and Jacob Marley were business partners. All they cared about was making money – they were not bothered that no one liked them. At the beginning of the story, Jacob Marley has died. Scrooge continues in his mean, grasping ways until he is visited by the ghost of his dead partner.

• The extract can be read to the class by the teacher; aloud by individual children in turn, or in silence individually.

ICT

After reading

Use the panel prompts in the Pupil Book as the basis of a class discussion.

• What is the name of the Ghost?
The name of the the the ghost is Jacob Marley.

• Who is he haunting?
He is haunting Scrooge.

• Why did the Ghost make 'a frightful cry' and shake his chain?
Scrooge said he didn't believe in him (the Ghost).

• What did the Ghost tell Scrooge to expect tomorrow?
The Ghost told Scrooge to expect the first of the Three Spirits.

• Explain the meaning of the words in bold.
ledgers: *business account books;* **phantom:** *ghost / spirit;* **incredulous:** *not able to believe;* **caustic:** *sarcastic / biting;* **swoon:** *faint;* **apparition:** *ghost / spirit;* **forbearance:** *patience in difficult situations;* **shun:** *avoid.*

• How does Scrooge feel about the Ghost:
a when it first appears?
b at the end of the extract?
At the start, he does not believe in the Ghost; by the end he does.

• Why do you think the Ghost has to drag the chain around with him?
Answers suggesting that the chain is a punishment. It is made of all the things he most cared about in life when he should have been caring about other people.

29

Hamlet, Prince of Denmark

The King has died suddenly and mysteriously. The Queen has married her dead husband's brother who has now become King. Prince Hamlet is very unhappy about his father's death and his mother's remarriage.

One bitterly cold winter night, on the wind-swept battlements of the royal castle at Elsinore the sentries were changing guard. Except for their shouts as they challenged each other and the muffled thunder of the sea on the rocks below, all was quiet; not a mouse was stirring.

Suddenly the sound of footsteps briskly marching …

'Halt! Who goes there?' cried Bernardo, the relief officer, as a figure rose up in front of him. He was so nervous that he had forgotten to wait to be challenged first.

'No, *you* answer *me*! Give me the password,' came the answer.

"Long live the King."'

'Are you Bernardo?'

'Yes.'

'You're very punctual.'

'It's past midnight, Francisco. Get to bed. Horatio and Marcellus are sharing the watch with me. If you see them, tell them to hurry.'

'I can hear them coming – here they are,' said Francisco. And when he had challenged and greeted the two newcomers, he lowered his pike. Wishing them good night, he marched off down the rocky path to the barracks, relieved that his freezing watch was over and quite unaware that anything unusual had happened to disturb Bernardo.

'Has this ghost appeared again?' said Horatio, half jokingly.

'I have seen nothing,' said Bernardo.

'Horatio thinks we have only imagined it,' said Marcellus. 'He won't believe we have both seen it twice. That's why I have asked him to share our watch tonight in case it appears again.'

'Nonsense. I'm sure it won't appear,' said Horatio, who was too matter-of-fact and level-headed to be superstitious.

'Last night, at the stroke of one –' Bernardo began, then broke off abruptly.

A tall majestic figure had loomed out of the darkness and stood before them, shimmering in the moonlight. Armed from head to foot, the helmet visor raised, it had a pale and haggard face and grizzled beard and seemed to be floating in the air.

'It's like our dead King,' Bernardo gasped.

'Exactly like him,' agreed Horatio, harrowed with fear and wonder.

He steadied his nerves and strode boldly forward. Holding his sword in front of him hilt upwards like a cross, he tried to question it. But it stalked away into the shadows as if it had been offended.

What could this vision mean? Clad in the same armour he had worn in the Norwegian war, it was the very image of the dead King. Why had he returned to haunt them? Could it be because the Norwegians, defeated in the recent war, were threatening to attack again and recover the land they had lost? As they paced up and down, Horatio and the two officers anxiously discussed these questions but could find no answer.

Suddenly, when the night was almost over, the ghost appeared again. Horatio stood in its path and challenged it. It seemed about to speak some message, when in the distance a cock crowed. Then it turned its head and began to drift away.

They cried out; they tried to trap it, to strike it with their pikes, but it melted into the shadows and all they struck was empty air.

Already the first gleams of dawn had splashed the eastern hills. Their watch over, the three soldiers left the battlements and returned to the palace, determined to tell Hamlet what they had seen. Hamlet was the dead King's son. Perhaps the ghost, who had been dumb to them, would speak to him.

The Enchanted Island, Ian Serraillier

Understanding the extract

- What is the setting for the extract?
- Who are the characters?
- What unusual thing have two of the soldiers seen?
- What happened when Horatio 'tried to question it'?
- When they left the battlements, what were the three soldiers going to do?

Looking at words

Explain the meaning of these words as they are used in the extract.

a battlements	b punctual	c pike
d level-headed	e superstitious	f majestic
g haggard	h harrowed	i dumb

Exploring further

- Why do you think the ghostly scene is set 'One bitterly cold winter night'?
- What impression do you get of Horatio?
- Why do you think that Horatio held his sword up 'like a cross'?
- Why do you think the ghost 'began to drift away' when 'a cock crowed'?
- Why do you think the ghost keeps appearing on the battlements?

Extra

Make the extract into a playscript and prepare it for performance.

Remember, you will need:

The scene; the characters; dialogue; stage directions that 'tell the story'; stage directions that tell the actors how to speak and what to do.

time; **c pike:** *a spear with a steel head;* **d level-headed:** *calm / sensible;* **e superstitious:** *believing in the power of magic;* **f majestic:** *magnificent / noble;* **g haggard:** *thin and care-worn;* **h harrowed:** *greatly distressed / upset;* **i dumb:** *would not speak.*

Exploring further

● Why do you think the ghostly scene is set 'One bitterly cold winter night'?
Answers suggesting the scene adds to the atmosphere of fear that the writer wants to create. The appearance of the ghost is much more frightening than it would be, say, on a bright sunny day.

● What impression do you get of Horatio?
Answers suggesting that he is not superstitious: 'too matter-of-fact and level-headed'; he is brave: 'He steadied his nerves and strode boldly forward', 'stood in its path and challenged it'.

● Why do you think that Horatio held his sword up 'like a cross'?
Answers suggesting he thought the ghost was evil and that he would be protected by the 'cross'.

● Why do you think the ghost 'began to drift away' when 'a cock crowed'?
Answers suggesting ghosts traditionally haunt in the night and have to return to where they have come from during daylight.

● Why do you think the ghost keeps appearing on the battlements?
Individual answers. Pupils may need to be reminded of the introduction. Can they make a connection between the ghost, the King's sudden death, and the remarriage?

ICT

Reading

The extract can be read to the class by the teacher, by individuals in the class or as a group.

Discussion group

In groups, pupils discuss the questions and make notes on their responses. Ensure pupils understand that they do not always have to agree.

Understanding the extract

● What is the setting for the extract?
'One bitterly cold winter night, on the wind-swept battlements of the royal castle at Elsinore'.

● Who are the characters?
Francisco: the sentry on watch; Bernardo: the relief sentry; Horatio and Marcellus: sharing the watch with Bernardo; the Ghost.

● What unusual thing have two of the soldiers seen?
Two of the soldiers have seen a ghost.

● What happened when Horatio 'tried to question it'?
'When Horatio tried to question it 'it stalked away into the shadows as if it had been offended.'

● When they left the battlements, what were the three soldiers going to do?
They were going to tell Hamlet what they had seen.

Looking at words

Explain the meaning of these words as they are used in the extract.
a battlements: *a wall on top of the castle;* **b punctual:** *on*

TEACH continued …

● What do you think the Ghost means when he says, 'It is required of every man that the spirit within him should walk abroad among his fellow-men'?
Answers suggesting that every man has a duty to care about and help other people, not just themselves.

● What do you think Scrooge means when he says that Jacob was 'a good man of business'?
Answers suggesting that Jacob was good at making money.

● In your own words, explain why you think Scrooge is being haunted.
Individual answers. Pupils should show an understanding of why Marley is being punished and that he is trying to help Scrooge avoid the same fate.

Plenary

If pupils know the story, ask them to relate what happens. If they don't know the story, ask them to predict what might happen.

TALK

Before reading

● Ask pupils to recap on why Marley haunted Scrooge (to warn him to change his ways), and ask pupils if they can think of any other reason why a ghost might haunt someone.

● Explain to pupils that they are going to read an extract from *Hamlet*. It was originally a play by Shakespeare, but here it has been written as a story.

The Ghostly Girl

Mandy awoke suddenly in the night, trembling with fear. Moonlight flooded her bedroom with silver and shadow. It was only a dream, she told herself, only a dream. So why was she shivering in a warm bed?

A memory of the dream returned and she threw back the bedclothes and switched on the light. It had all seemed so real, and she'd never had a fright like that before.

She wrapped a dressing-gown around her and opened the door. The house was quiet, the passage in darkness, as she felt her way along the wall to her brother's room. She opened the door and closed it behind her, switched on the light.

Joe's room was full of aeroplane models, and she had to move carefully to avoid them. She sat on the edge of his bed and shook him hard; Joe was a heavy sleeper.

Presently, her brother stirred. 'What's up, then? Mandy ...'

'I had a nightmare, Joe. It scared me – I've got to talk to somebody.'

Joe was twelve, two years younger than his sister, and sturdy, with unruly fair hair. Mandy shuddered. 'It was horrid!'

Joe sat up reluctantly; he was still sleepy. 'What was it about?'

'I was walking along, through a mist, and all round me were ruins. It was nowhere I've ever seen, I'm sure of that. And then *she* came towards me, through the mist. Her feet didn't touch the ground – she just drifted along. I could see right through her, Joe. She was a ghost, a girl of about my age in a long dress, and with a pale face. Her mouth was moving as if she was trying to say something, but I couldn't hear what it was – like watching the old silent movies on telly. That's all, really, because I woke up. But it was so real.' She forced a laugh. 'I don't know why I was scared so much – it was only a dream.'

Joe rubbed sleep from his eyes and looked hard at his sister. 'You do look a bit white ... Still, I never heard of anyone dreaming a ghost before.' He sounded impressed.

Mandy stood up. 'I'll be all right now, Joe. Thanks for listening.'

She tiptoed back to her room, and it was a long time before she fell asleep.

A week later, Mandy dreamed again. She stood among the ruins of an old house and it was dark. The ghost girl appeared before her, rippling as if seen through water. She felt icy cold. The ghost drifted nearer and lifted an arm, reaching out a hand to touch her ...

Mandy awoke abruptly, soaked with sweat, her heart thumping wildly. She pushed bedclothes into her mouth to stop herself screaming. It was ridiculous, she thought, scared silly by a dream ...

At the breakfast table, her mother commented, 'You look off-colour, Mandy. Are you sleeping all right?'

Joe hastily swallowed a spoonful of cereal. 'Was it the dream again?'

Their father looked up from his newspaper crossword. 'What dream's this? First I've heard of it.'

'She dreamed a ghost,' Joe said proudly.

Dream Ghost, Sydney J Bounds

Understanding the extract

1 When did Mandy have the first dream?

2 Who did she go to talk to after the first dream?

3 What did the girl in the dream look like?

4 At what point did Mandy wake up:
  a in the first dream   b in the second dream?

Understanding the words

5 Explain the meaning of these words and phrases as they are used in the extract.
  a avoid   b nightmare   c unruly
  d reluctantly   e silent movies   f ridiculous

Exploring further

6 Find evidence in the extract to show how Mandy reacted to the first dream.

7 Why do you think Mandy told her brother about her dream but not her parents?

8 What impression do you get of Mandy?

9 How do you think Mandy's parents will react now that they know about the dreams?

10 Do you think Mandy was more or less frightened the second time she had the dream? Explain your reasons.

Extra

Think of as many reasons as you can for why Mandy is having this dream. Choose the one you think is most likely.

TALK continued …

Extra

One member of the group should be elected as scribe, but ensure all members contribute. Let the groups act out the scene for the rest of the class and discuss each performance.

Plenary

Discuss what pupils think Hamlet will do when he hears about the ghost. Explain that Hamlet does meet the ghost on the battlements. What do they think the ghost will say to Hamlet?

WRITE

Before reading

- Discuss the idea of recurring dreams. Have pupils ever had them?
- Why do they think people have recurring dreams?

Reading

- Explain to pupils that they are going to read an extract from a story called 'Dream Ghost'.
- The extract can be read to the class by the teacher, by individuals to the class or to themselves.

Questions

Pupils answer the questions individually, drawing on what they have learnt from previous class work (*Teach*) and group work (*Talk*) about the conventions of ghost stories.

? Answer guidance

Understanding the extract

1 Mandy had the first dream 'in the night'.

2 Her brother, Joe.

3 'Her feet didn't touch the ground – she just drifted along. I could see right through her … She was a ghost, a girl of about my age in a long dress, and with a pale face. Her mouth was moving as if she was trying to say something …'

4 a When the ghost was speaking but Mandy couldn't hear.
  b 'when the ghost drifted nearer and lifted an arm, reaching out a hand to touch her …'

Understanding the words

5 a *avoid*: to keep away from;
  b *nightmare*: a frightening dream;
  c *unruly*: hard to control;
  d *reluctantly*: unwillingly;
  e *silent movies*: early films that had no sound;
  f *ridiculous*: stupid.

Exploring further

6 Answers based on evidence: 'trembling with fear' / 'shivering' / needed company – ''I've got to talk to somebody'' / 'shuddered'.

---

7 Answers that suggest her brother would be a more sympathetic listener. Perhaps she thought her parents would think she was being silly.

8 Answers that suggest Mandy is sensitive enough to have been affected by the dream – 'It was horrid!'– but she tries to be sensible and not over-dramatic – 'She forced a laugh. ''I don't know why I was scared so much – it was only a dream.'''

9 Individual answers that may suggest her parents will be sympathetic, or they may dismiss her as being silly.

10 Individual answers suggesting why Mandy was more or less frightened the second time she had the dream. Pupils should compare the first dream ('trembling with fear' / shivering / went to see her brother) with the second dream ('soaked with sweat' / 'heart thumping wildly' / 'pushed bedclothes into her mouth to stop herself screaming'). They should also take into account that, in the second dream, the ghost was 'reaching out a hand to touch her'.

Extra

Pupils should think about possible motives for a ghost to appear, for example, as a warning (Marley) or in revenge (King Hamlet).

- Discuss the three extracts. In what ways are they similar? In what ways are they different?

Round-up

- Use answers to the 'Extra' activity as the basis of a class discussion.

What happens next

Pupils may then like to know that the 'dream ghost' was appearing to Mandy to warn her. Mandy and Joe go to stay with her uncle in Devon. They go with their cousins, Ben and Polly, to play in some ruins on the moors.

Mandy recognises the place from her dream. They are playing hide and seek and Mandy hides in the overgrown shrubbery. The ghost girl appears again and prevents Mandy from falling down an overgrown well.

A life less ordinary
▶ Understanding the structure of a biography

Emmeline Pankhurst

Emmeline Goulden was born in Manchester in 1858. Her father was a **self-made man** who had begun his working life as an office boy and had risen to be a successful businessman. Emmeline grew up in a typical Victorian household where the father was master.

When Emmeline was fourteen, she was sent to Paris for her education. On her return, she married Richard Pankhurst who was a **barrister**. In the following years she had four children: Christabel, Sylvia, Frank and Ada. Emmeline had been a dutiful daughter; it now seemed as if she had settled into being a **dutiful** wife and mother.

Her husband, however, was not like her father. He had very different ideas about the role of women and encouraged Emmeline to see herself as his equal. She soon realised, however, that although she was an equal to her husband at home, outside she was just like other women – a **second-class citizen**. Women could not vote or become Members of Parliament so they had no power to change anything.

Emmeline, with a group of **like-minded** women, formed the WSPU (Women's Social and Political Union) and began to demand that women had the vote. The main political parties showed little interest in giving women the right to vote, despite massive demonstrations outside the Houses of Parliament. At this point, Emmeline decided there would be a change of **tactics**.

Members of the WSPU smashed windows, burned postboxes and set fire to unoccupied buildings. Some of the women were arrested and sent to jail. Emmeline was jailed for the first time in 1908. Women prisoners began hunger strikes and were brutally force-fed. When their health was in danger they were released, only to be re-arrested when their health improved.

This state of affairs continued until the beginning of the First World War. With the men away fighting, women turned their attention to keeping the country going: working in factories and on farms, driving ambulances, and generally doing all the work that their absent fathers, husbands and sons could not.

By the end of the war, it was generally accepted that women should have a right to vote. Women over the age of 30 were given the vote in 1918, but it was not until 1928, the year of Emmeline's death, that all women were given the vote on the same terms as men.

- Where and when was Emmeline born?
- Where did she go for her education?
- Who did she marry?
- What organisation did she form?
- What did the organisation want?
- Explain the meaning of the words and phrases in bold.
- Explain, in your own words, the meaning of the phrase 'father was master'.
- In what way was Emmeline's husband's attitude to women different from her father's?
- Why do you think it was generally accepted that women should have a right to vote' at the end of the First World War?
- There are seven paragraphs in the biography. Say briefly what each one is about.
- How is the biography organised?
- Why do you think the writer has included photographs?

Extracts

Emmeline Pankhurst
Neil Armstrong
Louis Braille

Planning

Biography and autobiography

Objectives

Renewed Primary Literacy Framework Year 6

1 *Speaking*
• Use talk to explore ideas, topics or issues.

2 *Listening and responding*
• Make notes … and discuss how note-taking varies depending on context and purpose.

3 *Understanding and interpreting texts*
• Understand underlying themes, causes and points of view.

Assessment focuses

AF2 Understand, describe, select or retrieve information, events or ideas from texts and use quotation and reference to text

L4/L5 Increasingly and clearly identifies relevant points from across a text and supports them by reference to the text.

AF4 Identify and comment on the structure and organisation of texts, including grammatical and presentational features

L3/L4/L5 Increasingly identifies features of organisation at text level, and starts to comment on structural choices.

Scottish Curriculum for Excellence: Literacy

Listening and Talking

Finding and using information (third / fourth levels)
Makes notes and organises these to develop thinking, help retain and recall information, explore issues and create new texts, using own words.

Reading

Finding and using information (third / fourth levels)
Using knowledge of features of text types, can find, select and sort information and use this for different purposes.

TEACH

This unit presents three biographical sketches of people who 'made a difference'. Pupils are given the opportunity to investigate the common features of biographical writing, for example, background and chronology, and they may choose to use one of the sketches as a basis for further research and their own biographical writing.

Pupils will be given the opportunity to investigate autobiographical writing and make comparisons in Unit 7.

Before reading

• What do pupils understand by the term 'biography'?

• Why do they think people like to read biographies?

• What biographies have they read? Pupils may at first say they haven't read any, but articles in magazines, which deal with a part of a person's life, can be deemed a biographical sketch.

 Reading

• Investigate the idea of voting with pupils. What experience have they had, for example, class votes? Extend the discussion to voting for local councillors, MPs, etc.

• Explain that not everyone has always had the right to vote, and it was not until 1928 that women could vote. This biographical sketch is about Emmeline Pankhurst, who made it her life's work to get votes for women.

• The extract can be read to the class by the teacher, aloud by individual children in turn, or in silence individually.

After reading

Use the panel prompts in the Pupil Book as the basis of a class discussion

• Where and when was Emmeline born?
She was born in Manchester, in 1858.

• Where did she go for her education?
She went to Paris for her education.

• Who did she marry?
She married Richard Pankhurst.

• What organisation did she form?
She formed the WSPU (Women's Social and Political Union).

• What did the organisation want?
The organisation wanted votes for women.

• Explain the meaning of the words and phrases in bold.
self-made man: *someone who becomes a success by his / her hard work;* **barrister:** *a lawyer who works in high courts;* **dutiful:** *obedient;* **second class citizen:** *treated as if you are not as important as other people;* **like-minded:** *having similar interests and opinions;* **tactics:** *methods / plans for achieving something.*

• Explain, in your own words, the meaning of the phrase 'father was master'.
Answers that suggest that Emmeline's father was the boss in the house, and the person who members of the family obeyed.

• In what way was Emmeline's husband's attitude to women different from her father's?
Answers that suggest Richard Pankhurst 'had very different ideas about the role of women and encouraged Emmeline to see herself as his equal.'

Neil Armstrong

Neil Alden Armstrong was born on 5 August 1930 in Wapakoneta, Ohio, in the United States. His father worked for the Ohio government and the family moved around the state, and lived in twenty different towns. He was fascinated by aeroplanes from a very early age and was determined to get his pilot's licence.

In 1947, after leaving Blume High School, Neil went to Purdue University to study aerospace engineering on a navy scholarship. In 1949, he was called up to serve in the navy, and eighteen months later he was a qualified naval aviator. He served as a navy pilot in the Korean War and flew 78 combat missions.

Back in America, he completed his science degree in 1955. He then worked for NASA (National Aeronautics and Space Administration) from 1955 to 1971. During the following years he worked as an engineer and test pilot. He flew 200 different types of aircraft, including jets, rockets, helicopters and gliders.

He applied, and was accepted, for astronaut training in 1962. Three years later, in 1965, he was the Command Pilot for *Gemini 8*. It was launched on 16 March 1966. The purpose of the mission was to dock with an unmanned craft, *Agena*, in space, and it was successfully accomplished.

On 23 December 1968, Armstrong was chosen as the Commander for *Apollo 11*, the manned mission to the moon.

Apollo 11 was to orbit the moon, and the lunar module, called Eagle, was to land on the surface. Along with Armstrong, Buzz Aldrin and Mike Collins made up the crew. Mike Collins would remain in Apollo 11 while Armstrong and Aldrin landed on the moon in Eagle.

On 16 July 1969, *Apollo 11* was launched from the Kennedy Space Centre in Florida. On 20 July, Eagle touched down on the moon's surface. Neil Armstrong was the first man to walk on the moon and, as he stepped out of the lunar module, he said, 'That's one small step for man, one giant leap for mankind.'

Armstrong and Aldrin spent a total of 21 hours and 36 minutes on the moon collecting samples of rock and dust. *Apollo 11* returned to Earth, 8 days, 3 hours and 18 minutes after take-off.

Armstrong worked at NASA until, in 1971, he became Professor of Aerospace Engineering at the University of Cincinnati. He has received many honours for his historic moon landing, including the Presidential Medal of Freedom and the NASA Distinguished Service Medal.

Understanding the biography

- Where and when was Neil Armstrong born?
- What did he serve as in the Korean War?
- When he had completed his science degree, what job did he do?
- What happened in:

  a 1962   b 1966   c 1969?

Looking at words

Explain the meaning of these words and phrases as they are used in the biography.

a fascinated by   b scholarship   c aviator

d unmanned   e accomplished

Exploring further

- What three pieces of evidence in the biography tell you that Armstrong was interested in flying?
- Explain, in your own words, what *Gemini 8*'s mission was.
- Why do you think the astronauts collected samples of moon rock and dust?
- Explain, in your own words, what you think Armstrong meant when he said, 'That's one small step for man, one giant leap for mankind.'
- There are eight paragraphs in the biography. Explain briefly what each one is about.
- How is the biography organised?

Extra

Space travel is very expensive. It has cost America millions of dollars. Do you think money should be spent in this way or not? Explain your reasons.

- Why do you think it was 'generally accepted that women should have a right to vote' at the end of the First World War?
  Answers based on evidence: 'With the men away fighting, women turned their attention to keeping the country going.' Women had proved that they were essential members of society and were, therefore, entitled to the same rights as men.

- There are seven paragraphs in the biography. Say briefly what each one is about.
  Para 1: early years; Para 2: education / marriage / children; Para 3: her husband's and society's attitude; Para 4: WSPU is formed; Para 5: change of tactics; Para 6: women during the First World War; Para 7: women get the vote.

- How is the biography organised?
  The biography is organised chronologically.

- Why do you think the writer has included photographs?
  Answers suggesting the photographs give readers more information and bring the text 'to life'.

Plenary

- Discuss the change of tactics. Do pupils think Emmeline was right to use violence? Why? Why not?
- What impression do pupils get of Emmeline Pankhurst?
- If they could meet her, what questions would they like to ask her?

TALK

Before reading

- Discuss space travel with the pupils. What do they know about it?
- What do they know about the moon landing?
- What books / films / documentaries have they read / seen about space travel?

Reading

- Explain to pupils that after the Second World War, the Americans and the Russians began a 'space race'. For most of the time the Russians were winning the race: they put the first living creature into space in 1957 – Laika, a dog; the first man into space in 1961 – Yuri Gagarin; and the first woman into space in 1963 – Valentina Tereshkova. Both countries were working towards landing an astronaut on the moon, and the Americans got there first. This is a biographical sketch of the first human being to walk on the moon.
- The extract can be read to the class by the teacher, or by individuals in the class or as a group.

Discussion group

In groups, pupils discuss the questions and make notes on their responses. Ensure pupils understand that they do not always have to agree.

Understanding the biography

- Where and when was Neil Armstrong born?
  He was born in Wapakoneta, Ohio in the United States in 1930.

- What did he serve as in the Korean War?
  He served as a naval pilot.

- When he had completed his science degree, what job did he do?
  He worked for NASA (National Aeronautics and Space Administration).

- What happened in:
  a 1962?
  He was accepted for astronaut training.
  b 1966?
  Gemini 8 was launched. Armstrong was the Command Pilot.
  c 1969?
  Apollo 11 was launched and Armstrong walked on the moon.

Looking at words

Explain the meaning of these words and phrases as they are used in the biography:
a fascinated by: *strongly interested in / very keen on;* **b scholarship:** *his university fees were paid for (by the navy);* **c aviator:** *aircraft pilot;* **d unmanned:** *not carrying human beings;* **e accomplished:** *completed.*

Exploring further

- What three pieces of evidence in the biography tell you that Armstrong was interested in flying?
  Answers based on evidence: 'He was fascinated by aeroplanes' / 'was determined to get his pilot's licence' / studied 'aerospace engineering' at university.

- Explain, in your own words, what Gemini 8's mission was.
  Individual answers that explain that Gemini 8 had to dock with Agena (join up) in space.

Louis Braille

Louis Braille was born in 1809, in the small town of Coupray, near Paris. His father made harnesses and other leather goods, and one of the tools he used was an awl. This is a short pointed stick used to punch holes into leather.

Louis liked to watch his father at work in his workshop. When he was three years old, he was playing with an awl when his hand slipped and he injured himself in the eye. At first, the wound did not seem too serious, but it became infected and within a few days Louis was blind in both eyes.

In the years that followed, he attended the local school. He was a very bright pupil, but learning was difficult because he could not read or write; he could only listen.

At the age of ten he was sent to the Royal Institute for Blind Youth in Paris. Here, Louis learned to read from books with raised letters, but the system was not very successful as it was difficult to tell the letters apart. Also, the books were bulky and expensive. The school only had fourteen of them. Louis read all of the fourteen books but it took a long time to work out the letters, then the words, and then the sentences. He was sure there must be a way to make 'reading' with his fingers quicker and easier.

One day, a soldier called Charles Barbier visited the school. He had invented a system called 'night writing' that allowed messages from officers to be read by soldiers in the dark. The system consisted of raised dots and dashes. The soldiers had to learn what the dots and dashes represented, then they could run their fingers over them to 'read' the message.

Louis tried the code and, although it was much better than the bulky books, it was still very slow. The dashes took up a lot of space so very little could be written on each page. Louis spent a great deal of time trying to improve the 'night writing'. He wanted to make it less complicated and to get more words on a page.

In the school vacation he worked on the problem. The solution came to him by handling the very tool that had made him blind. He could use a blunt awl to make a raised dot alphabet. It consisted of up to six dots, arranged in different positions, to represent the letters of the alphabet.

He published his first Braille book in 1829 and by 1837 had added symbols for music and maths. His system, surprisingly, was not greeted with great enthusiasm, and it took many years before it was universally accepted.

a	b	c	d	e	f	g	h	i	j	k	l	m
n	o	p	q	r	s	t	u	v	w	x	y	z

Understanding the biography

1 Where and when was Louis Braille born?

2 What did his father do?

3 What happened to Louis when:

a he was three years old   b he was ten years old

c he was twenty years old?

Understanding the words

4 Explain the meaning of these words and phrases as they are used in the biography.

a harnesses   b infected   c bulky   d consisted of
e less complicated   f symbols   g universally accepted

Exploring further

5 In what ways do you think only being able to listen to your teacher and not being able to read and write notes would be difficult?

6 Explain, in your own words, how 'night writing' worked.

7 What impression do you get of Louis Braille from this biography?

8 There are eight paragraphs in the biography. Write briefly what each one is about.

9 How is the biography organised?

Extra

Using the illustration of the Braille alphabet, write your own name in Braille.

TALK continued …

- Why do you think the astronauts collected samples of moon rock and dust?
  Answers that suggest scientists wanted to study them to find out more about the moon.

- Explain, in your own words, what you think Armstrong meant when he said, *'That's one small step for man, one giant leap for mankind.'*
  Answers suggesting that the small step from the lunar module represented a huge leap forward in terms of achievement.

- There are eight paragraphs in the biography. Explain briefly what each one is about.
  Para 1: early years; Para 2: education and Navy service; Para 3: astronaut training and first mission; Para 4: astronaut training and first mission; Para 5: Commander of Apollo 11; Para 6: Moon landing; Para 7: on the moon and return to Earth; Para 8: after the moon landing.

- How is the biography organised?
  The biography is organised chronologically.

Extra

Groups could discuss the statement, make notes of ideas and give a presentation of their ideas to the class.

Plenary

- What impression do pupils get of Neil Armstrong?

- If they could meet him, what questions would they like to ask him?

WRITE

Before reading

- Discuss what pupils understand by 'braille'. If possible, have a Braille book for pupils to look at and feel.

Reading

- Explain to pupils that books written in Braille are used widely by blind and partially sighted people so that they can read. The Braille alphabet was the invention of one man who was determined to overcome his blindness.

- The extract can be read to the class by the teacher, by individuals to the class or to themselves.

Questions

Pupils answer the questions individually, drawing on what they have learnt from previous class work (*Teach*) and group work (*Talk*) about the common features of biographical writing.

Round-up

- If pupils could meet Louis Braille, what questions would they like to ask him?

- Discuss:
  a the similarities in the characters of the three people the pupils have read about;
  b the common features of the three biographical sketches.

ICT

Answer guidance

Understanding the biography

1 He was born in Coupray, near Paris in 1809.
2 'His father made harnesses and other leather goods'.
3 a He injured himself and became blind in both eyes.
  b He went to the Royal Institute for Blind Youth in Paris.
  c He published his first Braille book.

Understanding the words

4 a *harnesses:* strong leather bands that help an animal to pull;
  b *infected:* full of bacteria;
  c *bulky:* large / heavy / difficult to handle;
  d *consisted of:* was made up of;
  e *less complicated:* less difficult / easier;
  f *symbols:* signs or marks that stand for something else;
  g *universally accepted:* in use worldwide.

Exploring further

5 Answers that suggest you would have to rely on your memory / you couldn't go back and reread something / you couldn't use notes, for example, to revise.
6 Answers that explain that the dots and dashes stood for letters which the reader could 'feel' and work out what the message said.
7 Answers that suggest he was: clever – 'a very bright pupil'; imaginative – 'He was sure there must be a way to make "reading" with his fingers quicker and easier'; determined – a great deal of time trying to improve the "night writing".
8 Para 1: early years; Para 2: his injury; Para 3: local schooling; Para 4; Royal Institute for Blind Youth; Para 5: Charles Barbier and 'night writing'; Para 6: improving 'night writing'; Para 7: the solution; Para 8: the Braille system.
9 Chronologically.

Extra

Individual answers.

Painting a picture
▶ Understanding themes and recognising personification

The Brook

I come from **haunts** of coot and hern,
I make a sudden **sally**,
And sparkle out among the fern,
To bicker down a valley.

By thirty hills I hurry down,
Or slip between the ridges,
By twenty **thorps**, a little town,
And half a hundred bridges.

I chatter over stony ways,
In little sharps and trebles,
I bubble into eddying bays,
I babble on the pebbles.

With many a curve my banks I **fret**
By many a field and fallow,
And many a fairy **foreland** set
With willow-weed and mallow.

I chatter, chatter, as I flow
To join the brimming river,
For men may come and men may go,
But I go on for ever.

I wind about, and in and out,
With here a blossom sailing,
And here and there a **lusty** trout,
And here and there a grayling.

And here and there a foamy flake
Upon me, as I travel
With many a silvery waterbreak
Above the golden gravel,

And draw them all along, and flow
To join the brimming river,
For men may come and men may go,
But I go on for ever.

I slip, I slide, I gloom, I glance,
Among my skimming swallows;
I make the netted sunbeam dance
Against my sandy shallows.

I murmur under moon and stars
In brambly wildernesses;
I linger by my shingly bars;
I **loiter** round my cresses;

And out again I curve and flow
To join the brimming river,
For men may come and men may go,
But I go on for ever.

The Brook, Alfred Lord Tennyson

- Where does the brook come from?
- Where is it going to?
- When is the brook moving:
  - quickly
  - slowly?
- Explain the meaning of the words and phrases in **bold**.
- What human qualities is the brook given in this poem?
- If the brook was human, what sort of person do you think it would be?
- Why do you think the poet has used the sound words 'chatter', 'babble' and 'murmur'?
- Explain the meaning of the last two lines of the poem in your own words.
- Explain why you like, or do not like, the poem.

Extracts

The Brook Alfred Lord Tennyson
The River's Story Brian Patten
Coral Reef Clare Bevan

Planning

Poetry (the power of imagery)

Objectives

Renewed Primary Literacy Framework Year 6
1 Speaking
• Use the techniques of dialogic talk to explore ideas, topics or issues.
3 Group discussion and interaction
• Understand and use a variety of ways to criticise constructively and respond to criticism.
7 Understanding and interpreting texts
• Understand underlying themes, causes, points of view.

Assessment focuses
AF3 Deduce, infer or interpret information, events or ideas from texts
L3/L4/L5 Increasingly infers meaning based on evidence in text.

AF5 Explain and comment on writers' use of language, including grammatical and literary features at word and sentence level
L3–L5 Increasingly identifies and explains writer's use of language, and comments on its effect.

Scottish Curriculum for Excellence: Literacy
Listening and Talking
Understanding, analysing, evaluating (third / fourth levels)
Shows understanding by giving detailed, evaluative comments, with evidence, about the content and form of short texts.

Reading
Understanding, analysing, evaluating (third / fourth levels)
Can comment, with evidence, on the content and form of short texts, and respond to literal, inferential and evaluative questions and other types of close reading tasks.

TEACH

In this unit pupils are given the opportunity to read poems that use personification. Each poem gives a voice to an element of the natural world, enabling them to describe themselves and, in the case of 'The River's Story' and 'Coral Reef', to warn humans of the consequences of mistreating them.

 ### Before reading

• What do pupils understand by the term 'personification'?

• Why do they think writers give non-living things human characteristics in their work?

• Give and ask for examples such as 'the sun smiled', 'the sea raged', etc.

 ### Reading

• Explain to pupils that they are going to read a poem called 'The Brook', where the brook itself tells its life story. It was written in the 19th century.

• The poem can be read to the class by the teacher, aloud by individual children in turn, or in silence individually.

After reading

Use the panel prompts in the Pupil Book as the basis of a class discussion.

• Where does the brook come from?
It comes from 'haunts of coot and hern' (heron): the place where these birds live and feed.

• Where is it going to?
It is going 'to join the brimming river'.

• When is the brook moving:
  • quickly *'over stony ways'; 'into eddying bays';*
  • slowly? *'under moon and stars'; 'in brambly wildernesses'.*

• Explain the meaning of the words and phrases in bold.
brook: *small stream;* **haunts:** *places where people or animals are usually found;* **sally:** *a quick burst of activity;* **thorps:** *an old-fashioned name for villages;* **in little sharps and trebles:** *sounding like musical notes;* **fret:** *wear away;* **foreland:** *a piece of land;* **lusty:** *healthy and strong;* **loiter:** *hang about / linger.*

• What human qualities is the brook given in this poem?
Answers that suggest that it can talk / think / decide on its movement and actions.

• If the brook was human, what sort of person do you think it would be?
Answers suggesting that it would be cheerful / energetic / determined.

• Why do you think the poet has used the sound words 'chatter', 'babble' and 'murmur'?
Answers that suggest the words 'copy' the actual sound: they are onomatopoeic, and 'chatter' and 'murmur' are usually associated with what humans do.

ICT

• Explain the meaning of the last two lines of the poem in your own words.
Individual answers suggesting that the brook is older than any human.

• Explain why you like, or do not like, this poem.
Individual answers.

The River's Story

I remember when life was good.
I shilly-shallied across meadows,
Tumbled down mountains,
I laughed and gurgled through woods,
Stretched and yawned in a myriad of floods.
Insects, weightless as sunbeams,
Settled upon my skin to drink.
I wore lily-pads like medals.
Fish, lazy and battle-scarred,
Gossiped beneath them.
The damselflies were my ballerinas,
The pike my ambassadors.
Kingfishers, disguised as rainbows,
Were my secret agents.
It was a sweet-time, a gone-time,
A time before factories grew,
Brick by greedy brick,
And left me cowering
In monstrous shadows.
Like drunken giants
They vomited their poison into me.
Tonight a scattering of vagrant bluebells,
Dwarfed by the same poisons,
Toll my ending.

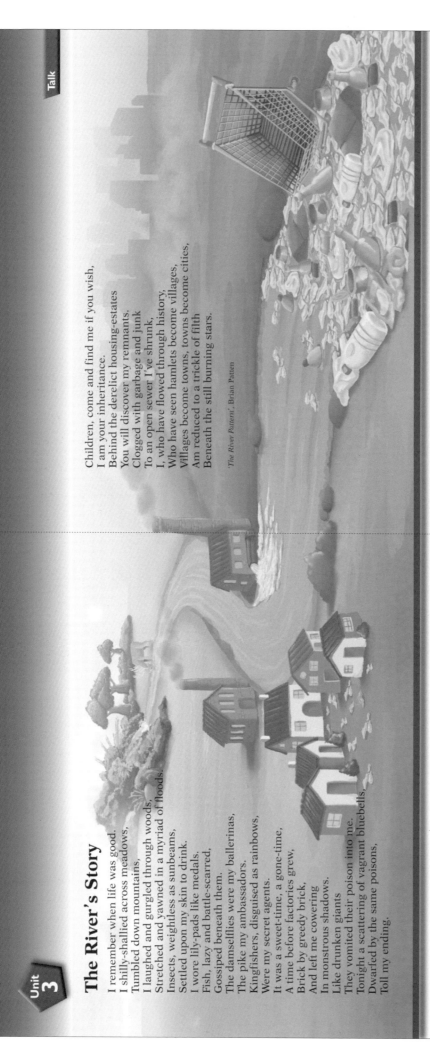

Children, come and find me if you wish,
I am your inheritance.
Behind the derelict housing-estates
You will discover my remnants.
Clogged with garbage and junk
To an open sewer I've shrunk,
I, who have flowed through history,
Who have seen hamlets become villages,
Villages become towns, towns become cities,
Am reduced to a trickle of filth
Beneath the still burning stars.

'The River Pattern', Brian Patten

Understanding the poem

- Where did the river flow 'when life was good'?
- Name three groups of living things associated with the river.
- What has happened around the river that has changed everything?
- What is now left of the river?

Looking at words

Explain the meaning of these words and phrases as they are used in the poem.

a myriad   b ambassadors   c cowering

d vomited   e vagrant   f Toll my ending

g I am your inheritance   h derelict   i remnants

Exploring further

- Why do you think the poet has made the river human?
- If the river was human, how do you think it felt when:
  a 'life was good'   b 'factories grew'?
- Why do you think the fish were 'battle-scarred'?
- What does the river mean when it says it has 'flowed through history'?
- What do you think 'The River's Story' is warning us about?

Extra

Using the information in the poem, make a poster to warn people about polluting our rivers. Write the text and illustrate the poster as if it was the river speaking.

TEACH continued ...

Plenary

- Use the pupils' answers to the final question as the basis for a class discussion.
- What do pupils think the poem would have lost or gained if it had just been a description of a brook by the poet?

TALK

Before reading

- The brook in the first poem gives the impression of being clean, flowing, fresh. Are all rivers like this?
- Do any pupils live near a river? What is it like?

Reading

- Explain to pupils that they are going to read a poem called 'The River's Story'. For some time this river is just like the brook in the first poem, but things go badly wrong.
- The extract can be read to the class by the teacher, by individuals in the class or as a group.

Discussion group

In groups, pupils discuss the questions and make notes on their responses. Ensure pupils understand that they do not always have to agree.

Understanding the poem

- Where did the river flow 'when life was good'?

It flowed 'across meadows', 'down mountains', 'through woods'.

- Name three groups of living things associated with the river.
  Any three from plants, insects, fish and birds.
- What has happened around the river that has changed everything?
  'factories grew'
- What is now left of the river?
  'a trickle of filth'

Looking at words

- Explain the meaning of these words and phrases as they are used in the poem:
  a myriad: *a great number;* **b ambassadors:** *representatives;* **c cowering:** *crouching / shrinking back;* **d vomited:** *poured forth / belched into;* **e vagrant:** *only there now and then;* **f Toll my ending:** *mark my death (like a bell at a funeral);* **g I am your inheritance:** *part of the children's future;* **h derelict:** *abandoned / not occupied;* **i remnants:** *remains.*

Exploring further

- Why do you think the poet has made the river human?
  Answers that suggest it makes what has happened to the river more terrible. If we think of the river as we would think of another human being it makes us realise how badly the river has been treated.
- If the river was human, how do you think it felt when:
  a *'life was good'* happy / contented;
  b *'factories grew'?* fearful / miserable / full of despair.

- Why do you think the fish were 'battle-scarred'?
  Answers that suggest they have been in fights with each other, or are scarred from fishing hooks.
- What does the river mean when it says it has 'flowed through history'?
  Answers that suggest it has been there for a long, long time.
- What do you think 'The River's Story' is warning us about?
  Answers that suggest we are being warned to take care of our natural resources / the planet.

Extra

Ensure each member of the group contributes ideas and has some input into actually producing the poster.

Plenary

- Discuss the pupils' posters. Encourage constructive criticism.
- In what ways are the brook of the first poem and the river similar, and in what ways are they different?

Coral Reef

I am a teeming city;
An underwater garden
Where fishes fly;
A lost forest
of skeleton trees;
A home for starry anemones;
A hiding place for frightened fishes;
A skulking place for prowling predators;
An alien world
Whose unseen monsters
Watch with luminous eyes;
An ancient palace topped by
Improbable towers;
A mermaid's maze;
A living barrier built on
Uncountable small deaths;
An endlessly growing sculpture;
A brittle mystery;
A vanishing trick;
A dazzling wonder
More magical than all
Your earthbound dreams;
I am a priceless treasure;
A precious heirloom,
And I am yours

To love
Or to lose
As you choose.

'Coral Reef', Clare Bevan

Understanding the poem

1 Find three things normally found on land that the coral reef says it is.

2 What do 'frightened fishes' use the coral reef for?

3 What choice do people have to make about coral reefs?

Understanding the words

4 Explain the meaning of these words as they are used in the poem.
  a teeming   **b** skeleton **c** predators
  d luminous   **e** brittle   **f** heirloom

Exploring further

5 Explain what the poet means when she says that the coral reef is:
  a 'built on / Uncountable small deaths'
  b 'An endlessly growing sculpture'

6 What do you think the 'unseen monsters' are?

7 Why do you think the towers are described as 'improbable'?

8 The poet has given the coral reef a voice. What warning is the coral reef giving to the reader?

9 If the coral reef was human, what sort of person do you think it would be?

Extra

Using what you have learnt from the poem, write briefly about why you think we should, or should not, protect coral reefs.

WRITE

Before reading

- Discuss what pupils understand by the term 'coral reef'.
- Where can coral reefs be found?
- What would you have to do to see a coral reef?

Reading

- Explain to pupils that they are going to read a poem called 'Coral Reef', where the reef itself describes what it looks like.

- The poem can be read to the class by the teacher, by individuals in the class or individually.

Questions

Pupils answer the questions individually, drawing on what they have learnt from previous class work (*Teach*) and group work (*Talk*) about the techniques of poetry, especially personification.

Round-up

- Use pupils' answers to the 'Extra' activity as the basis for a class discussion.
- Ask pupils which of the three poems they liked best? Why?

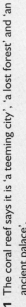 **ICT**

? Answer guidance

Understanding the poem

1 The coral reef says it is 'a teeming city', 'a lost forest' and 'an ancient palace'.
2 Frightened fishes use it as 'A hiding place'.
3 People have to decide whether 'To love / Or to lose' the coral reef.

Understanding the words

4 a teeming: full of life;
  b skeleton: (trees) made of bones;
  c predators: hunters;
  d luminous: bright / shining;
  e brittle: easily broken;
  f heirloom: something you inherit from the older generation.

Exploring further

5 a Answers suggesting that the coral reef is formed from the skeletons of numerous sea creatures.
  b Answers suggesting that as more skeletons are added, the coral reef grows into weird shapes as though it has been sculpted.
6 Answers that suggest large, fierce fish.
7 Answers suggesting that the towers are such amazing shapes that it seems difficult to believe they are real.
8 Answers suggesting the coral reef is warning that it will disappear if we do not look after it.
9 Individual answers.

Extra

Individual answers.

Monstrous creations
▶ Creating characters and building tension

Frankenstein

It was on a dark, sad night in November that I came to the end of my work. Most of what I had done had never been tried by anyone else before. It was quite impossible to get a perfect result from this first attempt. I had aimed at beauty, but the face of the creature I made was horrible. His skin was yellow, and hardly hid the muscles and **arteries** under it. His eyes were dull and the whites were almost the same colour as the yellow skin. The eyes were deep in his head. True, his hair was black and long, and his teeth were very white. But these touches of beauty only made the rest of his face appear more horrible.

His **limbs** were the right shape, but they were huge. One of the most difficult parts of the work was joining together the very tiny nerves and veins. Nobody had tried this before, and there were no scientific tools with which to do it. I had to work to a larger scale than normal, and I decided to make my creature eight feet high.

I looked down at this ugly thing, and was ill as a result. Often I had almost given up the worth it. I had driven myself on, and wondered whether all my hard work had been work, when I failed to do some particularly difficult part of it. But always I had started again. And here was the result of a year's work.

I felt certain that I could now bring my **creation** to life. The body was linked up with the wires and switches that would make use of electrical power to give it life.

As I looked at the ugly creation, I almost decided to destroy it and forget the whole idea. I wish I had. But I was not strong enough to turn away from the dream of being the creator of a race of beings who would serve me as their master. I wanted to use my great scientific powers to become a sort of god.

So I decided to carry on. A storm was building up over the city. I watched it and waited. Suddenly at about one in the morning, **the storm broke.** Within moments my mast was doing its work, and feeding down the power that I needed to put the spark of life into my creation. I watched, and moved the controls of my machines. Would it all work?

For some time nothing happened, and I began to wonder whether all my work had been **in vain.**

And then I saw the yellow eyes of the creature open. They moved from side to side. Then its chest began to move up and down and I could hear the steady beating of the heart. I fed in more power through the limbs, and the arms and legs began to jerk into life.

The creature began to move, and slowly sat up. I realized that it was even more horrible in life than it had been lying there with no life in it. My dream had been one of beauty, and instead I had created an ugly monster. My only wish was to escape from it, and I had no other thought in my mind. I ran out of the laboratory, and slammed the door behind me. I was full of **disgust** at what I had done.

Frankenstein, adapted by Patrick Nobes from the novel by Mary Shelley

- When does this part of the story take place?
- What did the creature look like?
- Why had the narrator almost given up the work?
- How did the narrator bring the creature to life?
- What did the narrator do when the creature 'slowly sat up'?
- Explain the meaning of the words and phrases in **bold.**
- Find evidence in the extract to suggest that the narrator was a scientist.
- Explain, in your own words, what the narrator's 'dream' was.
- In what way had he succeeded and failed?
- We know what the narrator feels when the creature comes to life. How do you think the creature feels?
- What do you think happens next?

After reading

Use the panel prompts in the Pupil Book as the basis of a class discussion.

- When does this part of the story take place?
  It takes place 'on a dark, sad night in November'.

- What did the creature look like?
  '... the face ... was horrible', '... skin was yellow', '... eyes were dull', etc.

- Why had the narrator *'almost given up the work'*?
  He had made himself ill, and when something was particularly difficult he felt like giving up.

- How did the narrator bring the creature to life?
  The narrator used 'electrical power'.

- What did the narrator do when the creature *'slowly sat up'*?
  The narrator 'ran out of the laboratory'.

- Explain the meaning of the words and phrases in bold.
  arteries: tubes that carry blood around the body; limbs: arms and legs; creation: what has been made; the storm broke: the storm began; in vain: without success; disgust: revulsion / hatred of what he had done.

- Find evidence in the extract to suggest that the narrator was a scientist.
  The narrator refers to 'scientific tools' and 'the laboratory'.

- Explain, in your own words, what the narrator's 'dream' was.
  Answers suggesting that he wanted to be as powerful as a god and make creatures that would obey him.

In this unit pupils are given the opportunity to investigate the enduring appeal of 'monsters' in fiction. While not actually a genre in themselves, monsters play a large part in fantasy and science fiction writing. In two of the extracts, the monsters are created by man. In the other, the monster is a creature of the earth.

Before reading

- Can pupils give examples of books/films that have monsters?

- Why do they think stories/films about monsters are so popular?

- Have pupils heard of Frankenstein? What do they know about him? (Correct the popular misconception that Frankenstein is the monster. He is the doctor who created the monster.)

Reading

- Explain to the pupils that they are going to read an extract from *Frankenstein*, a novel published in 1818.

- The story so far: Victor Frankenstein grew up in Switzerland with his parents and their adopted daughter, Elizabeth. Victor went to university to study science and became interested in creating human life. The extract begins when Victor has made his creature and tries to bring it to life.

- The extract can be read to the class by the teacher, aloud by individual children in turn, or in silence individually.

TEACH

Extracts

Frankenstein Mary Shelley (adapted by Patrick Nobes)
The Earth Giant Melvin Burgess
Jurassic Park Michael Crichton (adapted by Gail Herman)

Planning

Fiction genres: fantasy and science fiction

Objectives

Renewed Primary Literacy Framework Year 6

1 Speaking
• Use talk to explore ideas, topics or issues.
3 Group discussion and interaction
• Understand and use a variety of ways to criticise and respond to criticism.
8 Engaging with and responding to texts
• Compare how writers from different times and places present experiences and use language.

Assessment focuses

AF3 Deduce, infer and interpret information, events and ideas from texts
L4–L5 Increasingly make inferences and deductions based on evidence across a text.

AF5 Explain and comment on writers' use of language, including grammatical and literary features
L3/L4/L5 Increasingly identifies use of language and starts to comment on language choice.

Scottish Curriculum for Excellence: Literacy

Listening and Talking
Understanding, analysing, evaluating (third / fourth levels)
Responds to literal, inferential, evaluative and other types of questions; asks different kinds of questions; comments with evidence on content and form of short texts.

Reading
Understanding, analysing, evaluating (third / fourth levels)
Shows understanding across different areas of learning, identifies and considers the purpose and main ideas of a text and uses supporting detail; makes inferences from key statements.

The Earth Giant

One night, there is a great storm. Amy and her brother, Peter, hear a terrible noise like a dying giant, and a great oak is ripped out of the ground half a mile away. There Amy is sure there is something under that tree and goes to find out what.

She moved to another spot and began again but she uncovered only stones and roots. She tried again and again. All her senses told her there was something here, but the clay was completely dead.

At last she gave up and sat unhappily in the crater. She felt like crying. It was all wrong!

Then, slowly into her mind came a cold, vast presence: the huge ball of clay and roots the tree had torn from the ground. She turned her head to look up at it. It towered above her into the sky. It was difficult to think such a huge object had been underground all the time; it seemed somehow vaster than the ground. And then Amy realised. What she was looking for – what had called her – wasn't underground anymore. It was where it had always been – held in the embrace of the roots of the old oak. Only now it was high up over her head ...

Amy scrambled up out of the hole and began to toil up the cliff face of roots, clay and stones. She wasn't good at climbing but she was confident now. She knew where to go. She found a great broken root sticking out and sat on that, and she began to scrape.

The clay fell away in sticky clumps at first, but after the first layer it got harder. The earth and stones were packed so tightly together. She would have liked to dig with a stick, but she didn't dare. She might hurt something. Then she began to panic that Peter might come back and see and she began to shovel with both her hands as fast as she could, breaking her nails and tearing her skin. At last, she found what she was looking for:

It was almost the same colour as the earth, a deep reddish colour. It was smooth and shiny and only slightly warmer than the earth. Amy brushed it with her hand. It was round and firm. No one else would have recognised it, but Amy knew. It was part of an arm.

She moved a little further up the cliff of broken roots and began again. She dug the clay and stones away in handfuls, revealing the skin closer towards the neck. There was a pattern on it, where gravel and little stones had pressed into it over the years. A few more handfuls and the neck and the strong curve towards the shoulder came into view. Then, pressed firmly in the earth, the edge of an ear.

Amy stared. It had been a dream but it was real. She touched the skin on the ear gently with her finger. The skin was cold but Amy also knew it was not dead. It was the cold of someone, a woman or girl, who had been asleep for a long, long time – since before the old oak tree was an acorn. She had been asleep for hundreds or thousands of years, and now she was awakening again. There was no movement; the sleeper lay as still as the stones around her. Amy slowly stroked her neck and began to imagine it was getting warmer. It was only the heat of her own hand. Now she began to realise that everything was so big – the shoulder so long and high, the arm so broad. She was almost twice as big as a grown-up.

It was a giant in the earth.

The Earth Giant, Melvin Burgess

Understanding the extract

- What had ripped the oak tree out of the ground?
- Amy couldn't find what she was looking for in the ground. Where was it?
- Why didn't Amy want to use a stick to dig with?
- What did Amy discover?

Looking at words

Explain the meaning of these words as they are used in the extract.

a crater   b embrace   c toil
d confident   e recognised   f revealing

Exploring further

- Find evidence in the extract that suggests how Amy knew that 'something' was buried under the oak tree.
- How had the crater been made?
- Why do you think Amy began to 'imagine' it was getting warmer?
- How do you think Amy felt when she discovered the earth giant?
- What do you think happened next?

Extra

If you could talk to the earth giant, what questions would you ask?

• In what way had he succeeded and failed?
He succeeded as he made the creature and brought it to life. He failed because he wanted to create something beautiful but the monster was hideous.

• We know what the narrator feels when the creature comes to life. How do you think the creature feels?
Answers suggesting that the creature would be confused / frightened. (There is nothing to suggest that it would be aggressive or violent.)

• What do you think happens next?
Individual answers that take into account that Frankenstein cannot 'uncreate' his monster and he cannot stay away from the laboratory forever.

 Plenary

• Discuss whether pupils think Frankenstein was right or wrong to create his monster. Do they think the story will end sadly or happily? Why?

TALK

Before reading

• What do pupils understand by the term 'giant'?

• Is the term only used for someone who is very tall or are there other uses? (For example, people of exceptional courage or ability can be referred to as 'giants'.)

Reading

• Explain to pupils that they are going to read

an extract from a book called *The Earth Giant*, where Amy makes a remarkable discovery.

• The extract can be read to the class by the teacher, by individuals in the class or as a group.

 **Discussion group**

In groups, pupils discuss the questions and make notes on their responses. Ensure pupils understand that they do not always have to agree.

Understanding the extract

• What had ripped the oak tree out of the ground?
A great storm.

• Amy couldn't find what she was looking for in the ground. Where was it?
It was in the roots of the tree that were up in the air.

• Why didn't Amy want to use a stick to dig with?
'She might hurt something.'

• What did Amy discover?
Amy discovered 'a giant in the earth'.

Looking at words

• Explain the meaning of the words in bold as they are used in the extract.
a crater: *bowl-shaped hole;* **b embrace:** *surrounded by;* **c toil:** *making slow progress in climbing;* **d confident:** *sure of herself;* **e recognised:** *known what it was;* **f revealing:** *uncovering.*

Exploring further

• Find evidence in the extract that suggests how Amy knew that 'something' was buried under the oak tree.

'All her senses told her there was something here', '... into her mind came a cold, vast presence', '... what had called her ...', 'It had been a dream ...'

• How had the crater been made?
Answers that suggest the storm uprooted the huge tree and the crater was left behind where the roots had been.

• Why do you think Amy began to 'imagine it was getting warmer'?
Answers that suggest she so badly wanted the 'creature' to be alive that she imagined she could feel it getting warmer.

• How do you think Amy felt when she discovered the earth giant?
Answers that suggest Amy was not surprised as she knew there was something there. She shows no fear.

• What do you think happened next?
Individual answers.

Extra

Ensure all members of the group contribute questions. One pupil can take notes.

 Plenary

• Use pupils' ideas for the 'Extra' activity as the basis of a class discussion.

• Ask pupils to compare Frankenstein's monster with the earth giant. In what ways are they similar and in what ways are they different?

Jurassic Park

John Hammond has recreated the world of dinosaurs on a remote island. These dinosaurs are not models – they are the real thing! He keeps them behind electric fences. He invites Dr Alan Grant to come and see them. John Hammond sends his grandchildren, Tim and Lex, and Dr Grant on a tour of the island in electric cars. Dr Grant and Ian are in one car, and Tim, Lex and Gennaro are in another. Suddenly the power fails, just as they are outside the Tyrannosaurus paddock!

'Did you feel that?' Tim asked. At first Lex didn't know what he was talking about. But then she felt it, too. The car was shaking.

There were loud quaking sounds and it seemed as though the earth was moving – like something was taking giant footsteps.

Gennaro's eyes widened in fear. The sound got louder. The vibrations felt stronger. Whatever it was was coming closer. And then they all saw it. Tyrannosaurus rex. It was gripping the fence. Gennaro stared in horror. Oh no, he thought. The dinosaur should have felt an electric shock. The power must be out in the fences, too! But would it break through?

The T-rex swung its mighty head. Tim gasped. Its boxy head was bigger than Tim's whole body. And its body was bigger than a bus. The dinosaur waved its short, silly-looking arms in the air. Then it clawed the fence. The Tyrannosaurus was tearing it down!

All at once Gennaro bolted out of the car. He didn't say a word. He just ran, leaving Tim and Lex all alone. Lex began to scream. But Gennaro didn't stop. He raced towards a small building a short distance down the road. Moments later; he reached it and ran inside. But the building wasn't finished yet. Gennaro couldn't lock the wooden door behind him.

'What's he doing?' Ian asked Alan. They hadn't noticed the Tyrannosaurus yet.

Then they saw the fence come down. The Tyrannosaurus was free! It stood on the park road, eyeing the two cars.

'Don't move,' Alan whispered to Ian, 'It can't see us if we don't move.' The T-rex bent down. It peered through the car window at Ian. Ian froze. He couldn't have moved if he'd wanted to.

Suddenly the first car lit up like a beacon. Lex had turned on a flashlight. The dinosaur raised its head. It was drawn to the light.

'I'm sorry, sorry, sorry,' Lex mumbled to Tim as the T-rex thudded closer. It lifted its head high. Tim and Lex could see it through the sunroof.

Roar! The dinosaur opened its mouth wide, then roared again. It was so loud, the car windows rattled.

Then the T-rex struck.

The dinosaur lifted its powerful leg. Smash! It kicked the car. Windows shattered, and the car tilted on its side. The dinosaur lowered its head and butted the car off the road.

Inside, Tim and Lex tumbled about as the car rolled over. Now it was upside down. Tim twisted around to look out the window. They were right by the cliff.

The T-rex towered over the car. It put one leg on the frame and tore at the undercarriage of the car with its jaws. Biting at anything it could get a hold of, it ripped the rear axle free, tossed it aside, and bit a tyre. Lex and Tim were trapped. And the dinosaur was about to push them over the cliff!

Jurassic Park, adapted by Gail Herman from the novel by Michael Crichton

Understanding the extract

1 What has John Hammond done?
2 Where are the characters at the beginning of the extract?
3 Why could the T-rex grip the fence?
4 What does Gennaro do when he sees the T-rex?
5 Why does Alan say, 'Don't move'?

Understanding the words

6 Explain the meaning of these words as they are used in the extract.

a quaking   b vibrations   c bolted
d beacon   e butted   f undercarriage

Exploring further

7 How does the author create a feeling of fear in the first three paragraphs?
8 What impression do you get of Gennaro?
9 How do you know that Dr Alan Grant knows something about dinosaurs?
10 Why do you think Lex turned on the flashlight?

Extra

Imagine you are Tim or Lex. Rewrite the extract from your point of view.
Remember!

- You don't know what Alan and Ian are doing.
- You only know what is happening in your car and what you can see through the windows.
- Include your thoughts and feelings as you tell the story.

Before reading

- Discuss what pupils understand by the term 'Jurassic'.

- Elicit/explain that this is the name given to a time when dinosaurs roamed the earth.

- Have pupils seen the film *Jurassic Park?* If so, what did they think of it?

Reading

- Explain to the pupils that they are going to read an extract from a book called *Jurassic Park* on which the film was based.

- The extract can be read to the class by the teacher, by individuals in the class or individually.

Questions

Pupils answer the questions individually, drawing on what they have learnt from previous class work (*Teach*) and group work (*Talk*) about 'monsters' in fiction.

Round-up

- Discuss the three monsters that the pupils have read about.

- Are they all frightening?

- Which of the stories would they like to read? Why?

 ICT

? Answer guidance

Understanding the extract

1 He has 'recreated the world of dinosaurs on a remote island'.

2 They are touring the island 'in electric cars'.

3 The power to the electric fence was not working.

4 Gennaro 'bolted out of the car' / 'raced towards a small building . . . and ran inside'.

5 He explains that 'It can't see us if we don't move.'

Understanding the words

6 a *quaking*: shuddering;
   b *vibrations*: small backwards and forwards movements;
   c *bolted*: ran quickly (escaping);
   d *beacon*: a bright light to show where something is;
   e *butted*: hit with the head;
   f *undercarriage*: bottom part of a car.

Exploring further

7 Answers suggesting that in the first three paragraphs we are made aware of noise and movement but the dinosaur does not appear. The writer builds up the tension as we are waiting to find out what is making the 'quaking sounds' and causing the 'vibrations'.

8 Answers suggesting he is only worried about his own safety. He selfishly leaves the others to their fate. Also, he must be quite stupid if he thinks a 'small building' will protect him from a T-rex!

9 Answers based on the evidence: 'It can't see us if we don't move.'

10 Answers suggesting she was frightened in the dark with the creature outside and that it is a natural thing to want light when you are afraid. Perhaps she thought it might scare the dinosaur off.

Extra

Individual answers.

Unit 5

Which side are you on?

▶ Understanding the conventions of argument

Text messaging – good or bad?

Many adults are worried about the effect text messaging is having on the standard of written English of young people today. Others think that any form of **communication** between young people should be encouraged. So what are the advantages and disadvantages of text messaging?

Firstly, text messaging is a form of communication that young people are very **enthusiastic** about. Adults should not try to stop it just because they don't understand it and probably can't do it! They should realise that text messaging is spreading into the business world, so some adults see it as a very positive thing.

Another advantage of text messaging is that it is very fast. A text can be sent and replied to in a matter of seconds, almost like speaking face to face. There is no need to log on at a computer as is the case when sending an e-mail.

Perhaps one of the most important advantages for young people is that text messaging is a very private form of communication. Unlike a conversation or telephone call that can be **overheard**, a text can be read just by the person it is sent to, unless he or she chooses to show it to others. The reply is equally private.

There are, however, serious disadvantages creeping into the rules of text messaging into written English. Parents and teachers have seen the symbols and abbreviations of text messaging in their children's school work.

Spelling is an obvious problem. It is a fact that some young children are **convinced** that text spelling is correct, for example that 'great' is always 'gr8', whether texting or writing. Vowels are usually missed out altogether.

Punctuation is another area of **concern**. As it doesn't exist in the rules of text messaging, except to form symbols – for example, :) = I'm happy – it is fast disappearing from written work. Capitals have also changed their use in texting and stand for double letters in a word, instead of the beginning of sentences and proper nouns.

Text messaging is also having an effect on children's vocabulary. Messages are written in a kind of **shorthand** so children express themselves in **stock phrases** and come to rely on a very limited vocabulary, no matter what the situation.

So what is to be done? Banning text messaging is **unrealistic** and would stop a very valuable form of communication. Allowing the rules of text messaging to go uncorrected in written work would seriously affect the standard of children's education. The answer is to teach children 'appropriate' language. Just as they understand that the way they speak to friends is different from the way they speak to their parents and teachers, so we should help them to appreciate the different rules of text messaging and standard English. Neither one is right; neither one is wrong. It is only when they are used in the wrong way that the problems occur.

- What is the article about?
- According to the article, what are:
  - the advantages of text messaging
  - the disadvantages of text messaging?
- Explain the meaning of the words and phrases in bold.
- What do you think is the purpose of:
  - the first paragraph
  - the whole article?
- Who do you think is the intended audience?
- What do you think is the attitude of the writer to text messaging?
- Explain, in your own words, the conclusion the writer comes to. Do you think it is sensible or not? Explain your reasons.
- What do you think about text messaging?

Extracts

Text messaging – good or bad?
Animal testing
UFOs do not exist!

Planning

Understanding the conventions of argument

Objectives

Renewed Primary Literacy Framework Year 6

1 Speaking
- Use a range of oral techniques to present persuasive arguments and engaging narratives.

2 Listening and responding
- Participate in whole class debate using the conventions and language of debate, including standard English.

7 Understanding and interpreting texts
- Recognise rhetorical devices used to argue, persuade, mislead and sway the reader.

9 Creating and shaping texts
- In non-narrative, establish, balance, maintain viewpoints.

Assessment focuses

AF2 Understand, describe, select or retrieve information, events or ideas from texts and use quotation and reference to text

L3/L4/L5 Increasingly identifying relevant points in a text and supporting them by reference to the text.

AF6 Identify and comment on writers' purposes and viewpoints, and the overall effect of the text on the reader

L3/L4/L5 Identifies main purpose of text, starting to show awareness of writers' viewpoint and effect on reader.

Scottish Curriculum for Excellence: Literacy

Listening and Talking
Understanding, analysing, evaluating (third level)
Can distinguish fact from opinion and recognise influence.

Reading
Finding and using information (third / fourth levels)
Using knowledge of features of text types, can find, select and sort information and use this for different purposes.

TEACH

In this unit pupils are given the opportunity to investigate balanced and one-sided arguments on issues that arouse strong feelings, and to prepare their own arguments for debate.

Before reading

- What do pupils understand by the terms 'balanced argument' and 'pros and cons'?
- Elicit understanding or explain the terms indicating that a balanced argument considers all points of view, in other words, both the pros and cons.

Reading

- Explain to the pupils that they are going to read an article called 'Text messaging – good or bad?', which is an example of a balanced argument.
- The article can be read to the class by the teacher, aloud by individual children in turn, or in silence individually.

After reading

Use the panel prompts in the Pupil Book as the basis of a class discussion.

- What is the article about?
  It is about the pros and cons of text messaging.
- According to the article what are:
  - the advantages of text messaging?
    It is a very fast and private form of communication. Young people are very enthusiastic about it.
  - the disadvantages of text messaging?

ICT

The rules of text messaging are 'creeping into written English' causing problems with spelling, punctuation and limited vocabulary.

- Explain the meaning of the words and phrases in bold.

  communication: *the process of exchanging information through talking or writing;* **enthusiastic:** *keen;* **overheard:** *to hear a conversation that you are not involved in;* **convinced:** *sure;* **concern:** *worry;* **shorthand:** *a quick way of writing that involves symbols;* **stock phrases:** *a small number of phrases used repeatedly;* **unrealistic:** *not possible.*

- What do you think is the purpose of:
  - the first paragraph?
    To introduce the reader to what the article is about.
  - the whole article?
    To present the pros and cons (balanced argument) about text messaging.

- Who do you think is the intended audience?
  Answers that suggest the audience is probably an adult one.

- What do you think is the attitude of the writer to text messaging?
  Answers that suggest that the writer can see both points of view.

- Explain, in your own words, the conclusion the writer comes to. Do you think it is sensible or not? Explain your reasons.
  Answers suggesting that the writer thinks the advantages should be recognised, and the disadvantages dealt with by teaching 'appropriate' language: that there are different rules for text messaging and for written English.

Animal testing

When we are ill and visit the doctor or go into hospital, we expect that the drugs we are given or the operation we have to undergo to make us better are safe. Extensive research is done on these drugs and procedures in laboratories all over the world and, for some of this work, it is necessary to use animals.

Animal testing has been essential in making such procedures as heart, lung and kidney transplants, cataract operations and joint replacements viable. This means that humans can live longer and have a better quality of life. Reducing or banning animal testing would have serious consequences for the future of medical research and the benefits it brings to us.

Many people think that animal testing is not necessary. They claim that research can be done in other ways. This is not true. Wherever possible, scientists use other methods such as computer modelling and, as a result, the number of animals used in the last 30 years has halved. However, in many cases, these non-animal methods are not suitable. The only way for some medical advances to be made is through close study of how animals react to drugs and operations.

Scientists involved in animal testing do not do so lightly, and they are constantly striving to find alternative means to make drugs and medical procedures safe for humans. They follow a code known as the 'Three Rs':

- Replacement – to replace animal procedures with non-animal techniques wherever possible
- Reduction – to minimise the number of animals used
- Refinement – to improve the way experiments are carried out to make sure animals suffer as little as possible.

The use of animals in medical research is closely regulated. In 1986, The Animal Act was passed, and scientists have to prove that the cost of the research and the potential suffering of any animal involved are far out-weighed by the likely benefits to humans. A team of inspectors, who are vets or doctors, are employed by the government to ensure that all animal testing is done to these high standards.

That animal suffering occurs is not denied. But we have to ask ourselves a simple question. If we, or our loved ones, are faced with a life-threatening condition, do we not want medical researchers to have done everything possible to make the treatment safe and effective? Yes or no?

A survey by MORI in 2002 found that 90 per cent of the public accepted the need for animal testing provided that:

- the research is for serious medical or life-saving purposes
- there is no alternative
- there is no unnecessary suffering.

So, 90 per cent of the public said 'Yes'.

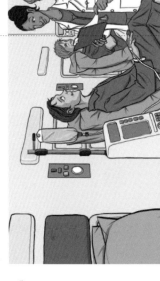

Understanding the article

- What is the article about?
- Explain briefly why the writer thinks animal testing is necessary.
- What has happened in the last 30 years?
- The Animals Act was passed in 1986. What does it make scientists do?

Looking at words

Explain the meaning of these words and phrases as they are used in the article.

a undergo	b procedures	c viable	d serious consequences
e striving	f minimise	g potential	h out-weighed
i effective			

Exploring further

- What is the purpose of:
  a the first paragraph   b the article as a whole?
- Who do you think is the intended audience?
- The writer says that the scientists involved in animal testing 'do not do so lightly'. What does this mean?
- A survey found that 90 per cent of the public agree with animal testing under certain conditions. Explain these conditions in your own words.
- Are you convinced by the writer's arguments? Why? Why not?

Extra

What arguments would you put forward to stop animal testing?

- What do you think about text messaging?

  Individual answers. Look for children to justify their opinion using reference to the text and personal experience.

Plenary

- Discuss the article with the pupils in terms of how fair they think the writer is.
- Can they think of any more advantages or disadvantages of text messaging?

TALK

Before reading

- What do pupils understand by the term 'animal testing'?
- Do they think it is right or wrong? Why?
- Take a vote on who is for and who is against animal testing before reading the article.

Reading

- Explain to pupils that they are going to read an article called 'Animal testing', where the writer is putting forward arguments in support of using animals in scientific experiments.
- The article can be read to the class by the teacher, by individuals in the class or as a group.

Discussion group

In groups, pupils discuss the questions and

make notes on their responses. Ensure pupils understand that they do not always have to agree.

Understanding the article

- What is the article about?

  It is about animal testing / using animals in scientific experiments.

- Explain briefly why the writer thinks animal testing is necessary.

  It is necessary to make drugs and medical procedures as safe as possible for humans.

- What has happened in the last 30 years?

  In the last 30 years '… the number of animals used … has halved'.

- The Animals Act was passed in 1986. What does it make scientists do?

  Scientists 'have to prove that the cost of the research and the potential suffering of any animal involved are far out-weighed by the likely benefits to humans'.

Looking at words

- Explain the meaning of these words and phrases as they are used in the article.

  *a **undergo:** have / experience; b **procedures:** medical treatments; c **viable:** possible / able to be done; d **serious consequences:** dangerous results; e **striving:** trying really hard; f **minimise:** reduce / make as small as possible; g **potential:** likely (in the future); h **out-weighed:** when one thing is more important than another; i **effective:** working well / producing the intended result.*

Exploring further

- What is the purpose of:

  a the first paragraph?

  To introduce the reader to what the article is about and show which side the writer is on.

b the article as a whole?

To put forward arguments to support animal testing.

- Who do you think is the intended audience?

  Answers that suggest the intended audience is those people who are against animal testing as it is trying to convince them that it is necessary.

- The writer says that the scientists involved in animal testing '*do not do so lightly*'. What does this mean?

  Answers that suggest they do so very seriously.

- A survey found that 90 per cent of the public agree with animal testing under certain conditions. Explain these conditions in your own words.

  Answers suggesting that people wanted to be sure that the reasons animals are used are serious (not trivial, such as for make-up); that there is no other way of getting results; and that the animal suffers as little as possible.

- Are you convinced by the writer's arguments? Why? Why not?

  Ensure all members of the group express their opinion.

Extra

Ensure all members of the group contribute ideas. One pupil can take notes of the discussion.

Plenary

- Use pupils' opinions about whether they are convinced or not of the writers' arguments together with the 'Extra' activity as the basis for a class discussion.

UFOs do not exist!

Strange lights in the sky! People claiming to have been abducted by aliens! The X Files and Independence Day warning us to be prepared to fight the 'baddies' from distant planets to protect our world! Well, maybe.

Let's look at the facts. These so-called unidentified flying objects are usually seen by very ordinary people, at night, and in lonely rural areas. They are almost always 'sighted' by a person on his or her own and no physical evidence is left to prove their story.

When UFOs were first 'sighted' in the 1950s, believers were convinced that Earth was being visited by Martians, Venusians, or other inhabitants of our solar system. When American and Russian space probes visited these planets and found them unable to support life, the UFO enthusiasts changed their minds and said that the 'aliens' must be from other galaxies! Their technology is so advanced they can travel faster than the speed of light to come and have a look at us.

But for what purpose? Suppose we say UFOs do exist. Suppose that we accept there are technologically superior beings who travel millions, if not billions, of light years to pay us a visit and then go away again. It doesn't make any sense. Why don't they make contact with our world leaders if they come in peace? Why don't they use their superior technology to take over our planet if they are not so peaceful? Why do they buzz around the countryside, allowing their spaceships to be seen by relatively few people, and then disappear again?

People will argue that it is not just the lone individual on a back road in the dead of night who claims to have seen strange lights in the sky, and they are right. Let's take the recent example of the 'four large glowing lights in the sky' that were reported by dozens of people from all over Wiltshire. So many people saw them, surely this is the proof we have been waiting for? Well, no. SUFOR – The Swindon UFO Research group – had to admit there was a very ordinary explanation. Cirencester College was open to the public that evening and they put on a light show that used powerful space tracer lights straight up into the sky. The light show stopped at 9.30pm and, not surprisingly, the sighting of the alien visitors stopped at the same time!

And finally – in the USA alone, five million people have claimed that they have been abducted by aliens in the last 50 years. That's 2,470 visits from UFOs every day. I wonder why I haven't seen one.

---

1 Where and when do UFO 'sightings' usually take place?
2 When were UFOs first sighted?
3 In the fourth paragraph, what is the writer puzzled about?
4 In your own words, explain what happened recently at Cirencester College.

Understanding the words

5 Explain the meaning of these words and phrases as they are used in the article.

a abducted   b rural   c physical evidence
d Venusians   e space probes   f superior technology

Exploring further

6 What is the purpose of:
a the first paragraph   b the article as a whole?
7 Who do you think is the intended audience?
8 The writer repeats the fact that most UFO 'sightings' are reported by people who are alone. What is the writer implying?
9 Does the writer want the final paragraph to be taken seriously or not? Explain your reasons.
10 Are you convinced by the writer's arguments? Why? Why not?

Extra

What arguments would you put forward to say that UFOs do exist?

- Take another class vote on animal testing. Has the article made any difference? If any pupils have changed their minds, can they explain why?

- Compare 'Text messaging – good or bad?' with 'Animal testing' and discuss similarities and differences.

WRITE

Before reading

- Discuss what pupils understand by the term 'UFO'.

- Take a class vote to see how many pupils believe there are UFOs and how many do not.

Reading

- Explain to pupils that they are going to read an article called 'UFOs do not exist!' by a writer who does not believe in them.

- The article can be read to the class by the teacher, by individuals in the class or individually.

Questions

Pupils answer the questions individually, drawing on what they have learnt from previous class work (*Teach*) and group work (*Talk*) about the conventions of argument.

- Conclude the unit by setting up a series of mini debates. Pupils work in pairs to propose or oppose a statement. Pupils can come up with suggestions and then be allocated a topic. Suggestions for suitable topics include: 'Children under 15 should not be allowed mobile phones'; 'Everyone should be a vegetarian'; 'Computers make people lazy'.

Round-up

- Use pupils' opinions about whether they are convinced or not of the writer's arguments together with the 'Extra' activity as the basis for a class discussion.

- Take another class vote on UFOs. Has the article made any difference? If any pupils have changed their minds, can they explain why?

- Ask pupils which of the arguments they have read are balanced and which are one-sided.

ICT

? Answer guidance

Understanding the article

1 UFO sightings usually occur 'at night, and in lonely rural areas'.

2 They were first sighted 'in the 1950s'.

3 The writer is puzzled about the UFOs' purpose in coming to Earth.

4 Answers should include: lights in the sky; seen by lots of people who thought the lights were UFOs; the college were having a light show; UFO sightings stopped when the light show stopped.

Understanding the words

5 a *abducted*: taken away against your will;

b *rural*: countryside;

c *physical evidence*: something that proves what people say is true (in this case, for example, part of the spaceship or something an alien was carrying or wearing);

d *Venusians*: beings who supposedly come from Venus;

e *space probes*: unmanned spacecraft that show scientists what a planet is like;

f *superior technology*: more advanced scientific knowledge and equipment.

Exploring further

6 a Answers suggesting that the purpose of the first paragraph is to introduce the reader to what the article is about, and to show which side the writer is on.

b Answers suggesting that the purpose of the article as a whole is to ridicule the idea of UFOs.

7 Answers that suggest the intended audience is those people who believe in UFOs.

8 Answers that suggest the writer is implying that these people are lying.

9 Answers suggesting that the writer does not want this to be taken seriously. The writer thinks it is ridiculous.

10 Individual answers. Look for children to justify their view using evidence from the text.

Extra

Ask the pupils to put forward individual arguments to say that UFOs do exist.

Finding a voice
(poetry dealing with issues)
▶ Exploring issues in poetry

The Loner

He leans against the playground wall,
Smacks his hands against the bricks
And other boredom-beating tricks,
Traces patterns with his feet,
Scuffs to make the tarmac squeak,
Back against the wall he stays –
And never plays.

The playground's **quick with life**,
The beat is strong.
Though sharp as a knife
Strife doesn't last long.
There is shouting, laughter, song,
And a place at the wall
For who won't belong.

We pass him running, skipping, walking,
In slow **huddled** groups, low talking,
Each in our familiar **clique**
We pass him by and never speak,
His loneness is his shell and shield
And neither he nor we will **yield**.

He wasn't there at the wall today,
Someone said he'd moved away
To another school and place
And on the wall where he used to lean
Someone had chalked
'Watch this space.'

'The Loner', Julie Holder

- Where and when is the poem set?
- What does the 'loner' do?
- What do the other children do?
- Where is the 'loner' at the end of the poem?
- Explain the meaning of the words and phrases in **bold**.
- Explain, in your own words, what you understand by the word 'loner'.
- What does the poet mean when she says 'And a place at the wall / For who won't belong'?
- Whose fault is it, do you think, that the 'loner' won't play with the others?
- How do you think:
  • the 'loner' feels about the other children
  • the other children feel about the 'loner'?
- What do you think the poet means by the last three lines of the poem?

Extracts

The Loner Julie Holder
Bullied Patricia Leighton
The New Boy John Walsh

Planning

Finding a voice (poetry dealing with issues)

Objectives

Renewed Primary Literacy Framework Year 6

1 Speaking
- Use a range of oral techniques to present persuasive arguments.
- Participate in whole-class debate using the conventions and language of debate, including standard English.

3 Group discussion and interaction
- Understand and use a variety of ways to criticise constructively and respond to criticism.

4 Drama
- Improvise using a range of drama strategies and conventions to explore themes.

7 Understanding and interpreting texts
- Understand underlying themes, causes, points of view.

Assessment focuses
AF6 Identify and comment on writers' purposes and viewpoints, and the overall effect of the text on the reader
L4 Comments simply on writer's viewpoint and overall effect on the reader.
L5 Identifies and can explain the main purpose, viewpoint and effect on the reader of a text.

Scottish Curriculum for Excellence:
Listening and Talking
Understanding, analysing, evaluating (third / fourth levels)
Shows understanding of the techniques of influence and persuasion.

Reading
Understanding, analysing, evaluating (third level)
Can identify the purpose and main concerns of a text, infer meaning, and identify and discuss similarities and differences between different texts.

TEACH

In this unit pupils are given the opportunity to read poems that raise issues. The connecting theme is 'school life' and the issues are such that many pupils will have witnessed or had experience of.

Before reading

- Discuss 'friendship' with the pupils.
- What makes us friends with some people and not others?
- Why do we like being part of a group of friends?

Reading

- Explain to the pupils that they are going to read a poem called 'The Loner', told from the point of view of a child who is part of a group but watches the child who is on his own.
- The poem can be read to the class by the teacher, aloud by individual children in turn, or in silence individually.

ICT

After reading

Use the panel prompts in the Pupil Book as the basis of a class discussion.

- Where and when is the poem set?
  The poem is set in the playground at playtime.
- What does the 'loner' do?
  The loner 'leans against the playground wall' / 'smacks his hands against the bricks' / 'Traces patterns with his feet', etc.
- What do the other children do?
  The other children argue ('strife') / 'There is shouting,

laughter; song' / They pass him 'running, skipping, walking' / they are in 'huddled groups', etc.

- Where is the 'loner' at the end of the poem?
  Somewhere else: 'He wasn't there at the wall today'.
- Explain the meaning of the words and phrases in bold.
  scuffs: *marks / wears down;* **quick with life:** *active / energetic;* **strife:** *argument / disagreement;* **huddled:** *standing close together;* **clique:** *small, exclusive group of people;* **yield:** *give in.*
- Explain, in your own words, what you understand by the word 'loner'?
  Answers that suggest someone is alone because they want to be or because no one wants to know them.
- What does the poet mean when she says 'And a place at the wall / For who won't belong'?
  Answers that suggest the boy refuses to join in.
- Whose fault is it, do you think, that the loner won't play with the others?
  It could be the boy's fault as he 'won't belong', although he could be shy, or it could be the other children who haven't tried to make friends with him.
- How do you think:
  - the 'loner' feels about the other children?
    Answers suggesting he may not care about them or he may be envious because he would like to be one of them.
  - the other children feel about the 'loner'?
    They probably don't care about him, except for the poet, who probably feels sorry for him.
- What do you think the poet means by the last three lines of the poem?
  Individual answers.

Bullied

Bullies get you.
I don't know how but they do.
They seem to have some
secret inborn radar
tuned in to loners,
quiet ones,
different ones.

You don't have to
do anything, say anything.
Seems you just have to be you.

Grown-ups think they know.
Bullies? Just cowards, they say,
*unsure of themselves,
needing to act big.*
But it's hard to believe
when jeering faces
zoom up to yours.

When they're hassling you,
calling you names,
leading the chanting,
the whispering,
urging the others on,
a relentless horde
of nagging, pecking birds.

Then there's the 'in-betweens',
the waiting, the not knowing,
just sure that
sooner or later
it's going to come.
The worst times;
the thinking times.

Don't ask me the answer.
I don't know but –
I'm getting there.

Keep my eyes skinned,
find a crowd to vanish into
before *they see me.*
Cornered, I know I can't look them
in the eye – but I've learned
not to look at the floor,
to try and walk tall.

Mostly I've learned
to talk in my head,
tell myself
*it's not me, I'm all right –
they're the idiots, the misfits.*
Eventually
it begins to sink in.

I'm getting tougher inside.
It's working.
Just don't give in.

Try anything, anything.
But don't *let* them win.

'Bullied', Patricia Leighton.

Understanding the poem

- According to the poem, who do bullies pick on?
- What does the poet say is the 'worst' time?
- What is the poet learning to do to avoid being picked on?
- What is she determined not to let happen?

Looking at words

Explain the meaning of these words and phrases as they are used in the poem.

a radar   b unsure   c jeering
d hassling   e relentless   f eyes skinned
g walk tall   h misfits   i sink in

Exploring further

- Explain, in your own words, what 'grown-ups' say about bullies.
- In the fourth verse, what does the poet compare bullies to? Explain why you think this is or isn't a good comparison.
- Why do you think the poet has learned 'not to look at the floor'?
- Why do you think it is important that the poet believes 'it's not me, I'm all right'?

Extra

Why do you think people bully other people?
What advice you would give to someone who was being bullied?

TEACH continued ...

Plenary

- Discuss what pupils think of the poem. How do they feel about the loner? If they had been one of the other children, what would they have done?

TALK

Before reading

- Have pupils ever been a victim of, or witnessed, bullying?

- Why do they think people bully other people?

- What do they think of bullies?

Reading

- Explain to the pupils that they are going to read a poem called 'Bullied', written from the viewpoint of someone being bullied.

- The extract can be read to the class by the teacher, by individuals in the class or as a group.

Discussion group

In groups, pupils discuss the questions and make notes on their responses. Ensure pupils understand that they do not always have to agree.

Understanding the poem

- According to the poem, who do bullies pick on?

  Bullies pick on 'loners, / quiet ones, / different ones'.

- What does the poet say is the 'worst' time?

  '... the in-betweens' are the worst time.

- What is the poet learning to do to avoid being picked on?

  The poet is learning to 'Keep my eyes skinned, / find a crowd to vanish into' / 'not to look at the floor, / to try and walk tall' / 'to talk in my head'.

- What is she determined not to let happen?

  The poet says 'don't let them win'.

Looking at words

Explain the meaning of these words and phrases as they are used in the poem:

a radar: *tracking device;* **b unsure:** *lacking in confidence;* **c jeering:** *taunting;* **d hassling:** *causing you trouble;* **e relentless:** *never stopping;* **f eyes skinned:** *be on the look out;* **g walk tall:** *head up, shoulders back, looking as if you have nothing to be afraid of;* **h misfits:** *people who do not fit in;* **i sink in:** *register / make sense.*

Exploring further

- Explain, in your own words, what 'grown-ups' say about bullies?

  Answers that suggest grown-ups say bullies are really cowards who need to show off and pick on others so people will think they are tough.

- In the fourth verse, what does the poet compare bullies to? Explain why you think this is or isn't a good comparison.

  The poet compares bullies to 'a relentless horde / of nagging, pecking birds'. Answers that suggest this is a good comparison as a group of birds with beaks and flapping wings is very intimidating and scary.

- Why do you think the poet has learnt 'not to look at the floor'?

  Answers that suggest looking at the floor is a sign of weakness that the bullies are 'tuned into'.

- Why do you think it is important that the poet believes 'it's not me, I'm all right'?

  Answers that suggest this is the first step to combating the bullies. If someone feels it is their fault that they are being bullied, it will keep happening.

Extra

Ensure all members of the group contribute ideas. One pupil can make notes of the discussion.

Plenary

- Use the groups' answers to the 'Extra' activity as the basis for a class discussion.

61

The New Boy

The door swung inward. I stood and breathed
The new-school atmosphere:
The smell of polish and disinfectant,
And the flavour of my own fear.

I followed into the cloakroom; the walls
Rang to the shattering noise
Of boys who barged and boys who banged;
Boys and still more boys!

A boot flew by. Its angry owner
Pursued with force and yell;
Somewhere a man snapped orders; somewhere
There clanged a bell.

And there I hung with my new schoolmates;
They pushing and shoving me; I
Unknown, unwanted, pinned to the wall;
On the verge of ready-to-cry.

Then, from the doorway, a boy called out:
'Hey, you over there! You're new!
Don't just stand there propping the wall up!
I'll look after you!'

I turned; I timidly raised my eyes;
He stood and grinned meanwhile;
And my fear died, and my lips answered
Smile for his smile.

He showed me the basins, the rows of pegs;
He hung my cap at the end;
He led me away to my new classroom ...
And now that boy's my friend.

'The New Boy', John Walsh

Understanding the poem

1 What is the setting for the poem?
2 What smells does the poet notice?
3 When the poet was 'pinned to the wall', what was he about to do?
4 When did the poet's 'fear' die?

Understanding the words

5 Explain the meaning of the following words and phrases as they are
   used in the poem.

   a atmosphere   b shattering   c pursued
   d on the verge   e timidly

Exploring Further

6 Find evidence in the poem that tells you how the boy was feeling at
   the beginning of the poem.
7 Find evidence that tells you how he was feeling at the end of the
   poem.
8 What impression is the poet trying to create with the words 'barged',
   'banged' and 'pushing and shoving'?
9 Do you think the boys were being deliberately unkind to the poet?
   Why? Why not?
10 There are 'Boys and still more boys' in the school. Why do you think it
   took only one boy being kind to the poet to make him feel better?

Extra

Imagine you had to move to a new school. Write about what you would
look forward to and what you would be worried about.

Before reading

- Have any of the pupils come from another school and been the new boy/girl in the class?

- How did it feel?

- How did the other children treat them?

- If none of the pupils have been in this position, ask them to imagine how it would feel.

Reading

- Explain to pupils that they are going to read a poem called 'The New Boy', which is told from the point of view of a boy who has started a new school where everyone else knows each other.

- The poem can be read to the class by the teacher, by individuals in the class or individually.

Questions

Pupils answer the questions individually, drawing on what they have learnt from previous class work (*Teach*) and group work (*Talk*) about the viewpoints in the poems.

 ICT

? Answer guidance

Understanding the poem

1 The setting is the boy's new school.

2 The poet smells 'polish and disinfectant' / 'my own fear'.

3 He was about to cry.

4 When another boy 'grinned' at him.

Understanding the words

5 a *atmosphere*: mood of the place;
   b *shattering*: ear-splitting;
   c *pursued*: chased;
   d *on the verge*: ready to;
   e *timidly*: fearfully.

Exploring further

6 At the beginning of the poem the poet was feeling scared: 'my own fear' / 'unknown, unwanted' / 'on the verge of ready-to-cry'.

7 At the end of the poem the poet feels happier: 'my fear died' / 'Smile for his smile' / 'that boy's my friend'.

8 Answers that suggest the poet is trying to create the impression of the noise and confusion the new boy found himself in.

9 Answers that suggest the boys were not being deliberately unkind. They were just behaving as normal and had not really noticed him.

10 Answers that suggest the new boy was feeling alone and frightened and only needed another person to take notice of him and help to make him feel better.

Extra

Individual answers

 Round-up

- Discuss the issues raised by the three poems.

- Ask pupils which of the three poems they liked best? Why?

- Conclude the unit by asking groups to dramatise a scene based on one of the poems and present it to the class. For example:

  – 'The Loner': one of the children could go up to the boy and try to get him to join in;

  – 'Bullied': the poet could stand up to the bullies;

  – 'The New Boy': a conversation between the new boy and the boy who befriends him.

Unit 7

Daring deeds
▶ Explore how writers present experiences

Endurance's Last Voyage

After long months of **ceaseless** anxiety and strain, after times when hope beat high and times when the outlook was black indeed, the end of the *Endurance* has come. But though we have been **compelled** to abandon the ship, which is crushed beyond all hope of ever being righted, we are alive and well, and we have stores and equipment for the task that lies before us. It is hard to write what I feel. To a sailor his ship is more than a floating home, and in the Endurance, I had centred ambitions, hopes and desires. Now, straining and groaning, her timbers cracking and her wounds gaping, she is slowly giving up her **sentient** life at the very outset of her career. She is crushed and abandoned after drifting more than 570 miles in a north-westerly direction during the 281 days since she became locked in the ice … We are now 346 miles from Paulet Island, the nearest point where there is any possibility of finding food and shelter. A small hut built there by the Swedish expedition in 1902 is filled with stores left by the Argentine relief ship …

This morning, our last on the ship, the weather was clear, with a gentle south-south-easterly to south-south-westerly breeze. From the crow's nest there was no sign of land of any sort. The pressure was increasing steadily, and the passing hours brought no relief or **respite** for the ship. The attack of the ice reached its climax at 4 p.m. The ship was hove stern up by the pressure, and the driving floe, moving **laterally** across the stern, split the rudder and tore out the rudder-post and stern-post. Then, while we watched, the ice loosened and the *Endurance* sank a little. The decks were breaking upwards and the water was pouring in below. Again the pressure began, and at 5 p.m. I ordered all hands on to the ice. The twisting, grinding **floes** were working their will at last on the ship. It was a sickening sensation to feel the decks breaking up under one's feet, the great beams bending and then snapping with a noise like heavy gun-fire …

Just before leaving, I looked down the engine-room skylight as I stood on the quivering deck, and saw the engines dropping sideways as the stays and bed-plates gave way. I cannot describe the impression of relentless destruction that was forced upon me as I looked down and around. The floes, with the force of millions of tons of moving ice behind them, were simply **annihilating** the ship …

South, Sir Ernest Shackleton

- Who is the author of the autobiography?
- What is the name of the ship?
- Where do they have to get to, to find food and shelter?
- At what time did they leave the ship and go on to the ice?
- Explain the meaning of the words in **bold**.
- Find evidence in the extract to show that Shackleton:
  • tried to be positive in this situation
  • was very upset about losing the ship.
- Find an example where Shackleton:
  • records a fact
  • expresses a feeling.
- What impression do you get of Shackleton?
- Do you think the extract gives a good impression of the awful situation Shackleton and his men find themselves in? Explain your reasons.

Extracts

South Sir Ernest Shackleton

20 HRS, 40 MIN ... Our Flight in the Friendship Amelia Earhart

Touching the Void Joe Simpson

Planning

Autobiography (Biography and autobiography)

Objectives

Renewed Primary Literacy Framework Year 6

1 Speaking
- Use talk to explore ideas, topics or issues.

2 Listening and responding
- Make notes ... and discuss how note-taking varies depending on context and purpose.

3 Understanding and interpreting texts
- Understand underlying themes, causes, points of view.

8 Engaging with and responding to texts
- Compare how writers from different times and places present experiences and use language.

Assessment focuses

AF2 Understand, describe, select or retrieve information, events or ideas from texts and use quotation and reference to text

L3–L5 Increasingly and clearly identifies relevant points from across a text and supports them by reference to the text.

AF5 Explain and comment on writers' use of language, including grammatical and literary features

L3/L4/L5 Shows increasing awareness of features of writer's language and comments on effects of these.

Scottish Curriculum for Excellence: Literacy

Listening and Talking

Understanding, analysing, evaluating (third)
Can recognise the difference between fact and opinion.

Reading

Finding and using information (third / fourth levels)
Using knowledge of features of text types, can find, select and sort information and use this for different purposes.

This unit presents three autobiographical extracts of people who embarked on dangerous exploits. Pupils are given the opportunity to investigate the common features of autobiographical writing, for example, first person account, past tense, facts, opinion and feeling, and can compare this text type with the examples of biographical writing in Unit 2.

Before reading

- What do pupils understand by the term 'autobiography'?
- Why do they think people like to read autobiographies?
- What autobiographies have they read? Pupils may at first say they haven't read any, but articles in magazines that are first person accounts about a particular aspect of someone's life can be deemed autobiographical writing.

Reading

- Explain to pupils that they are going to read an extract from Sir Ernest Shackleton's autobiography *South* and discuss what they know about the South Pole.
- Background information: Shackleton was a British explorer. He was born in 1874 and died in 1922. He accompanied Scott on his expedition to the South Pole in 1901–04, and his own expedition of 1908–09 nearly made it there. He tried again in 1914 on the ship *Endurance*, and it is from this expedition that the extract is taken.

- The extract can be read to the class by the teacher, aloud by individual children in turn, or in silence individually.

After reading

Use the panel prompts in the Pupil Book as the basis of a class discussion.

- Who is the author of the autobiography?
  Sir Ernest Shackleton is the author.

- What is the name of the ship?
  The ship's name is Endurance.

- Where do they have to get to, to find food and shelter?
  They have to reach Paulet Island.

- At what time did they leave the ship and go on to the ice?
  They left the ship at 5 p.m.

- Explain the meaning of the words in bold.
  ceaseless: *never ending / constant;* **compelled:** *forced;* **sentient:** *having the power of feeling (Shackleton regards his ship as a 'being' in its own right);* **respite:** *stopping (from ice crushing the ship);* **laterally:** *from side to side;* **floes:** *sheets of floating ice;* **annihilating:** *totally destroying.*

- Find evidence in the extract to show that Shackleton:
  - tried to be positive in this situation
    '... we are alive and well, and we have stores and equipment for the task that lies before us.'
  - was very upset about losing the ship.
    For example, '... in the Endurance, I had centred ambitions, hopes and desires.'

20 HRS, 40 MIN …
Our Flight in the Friendship

In 1928, Amelia Earhart was the first woman to cross the Atlantic by aeroplane. Along with Wilmer (Bill) Stultz and Louis ('Slim') Gordon, she flew from Trepassey in Canada to Burry Port in the United Kingdom.

Can't use radio at all. Coming down now in a rather clear spot. 2500 ft. Everything sliding forward.
8:50. 2 Boats!!!!
Trans steamer.
Try to get bearing. Radio won't work. One hr's gas. Mess.
All craft cutting our course. Why?

So the log ends.

Its last page records that we had but one hour's supply of gas left; that the time for reaching Ireland had passed; that the course of the vessel sighted perplexed us; that our radio was useless.

Where were we? Should we keep faith with our course and continue? Were we beaten? 'Mess' epitomised the blackness of the moment. We had to. With faith lost in that, it was hopeless to carry on. Besides, when last we checked it, before the radio went dead, the plane had been holding true.

We circled the *America*, although having no idea of her identity at the time. With the radio crippled, in an effort to get our position, Bill scribbled a note. The note

and an orange to weight it, I tied in a bag with an absurd piece of silver cord. As we circled the *America*, the bag was dropped through the hatch. But the combination of our speed, the movement of the vessel, the wind and the lightness of the missile was too much for our marksmanship. We tried another shot, using our remaining orange. No luck.

Should we seek safety and try to come down beside the steamer? Perhaps one reason the attempt was never attempted was the roughness of the sea which not only made a landing difficult but a take-off impossible.

Bill leaped to the radio with the hope of at least receiving a message. At some moment in the excitement, before I closed the hatch which opens in the bottom of the fuselage I lay flat and took a photograph. This, I am told, is the first one made of a vessel at sea from a plane in trans-Atlantic flight…

We could see only a few miles of water, which melted into the greyness on all sides. The ceiling was so low we could fly at an altitude of only 500 feet. As we moved, our miniature world of visibility, bounded by its walls of mist, moved with us. Half an hour later into it suddenly swam a fishing vessel. In a matter of minutes a fleet of small craft, probably fishing vessels, were almost below us. Happily their course paralleled ours. Although the gasoline in the tanks was vanishing fast, we began to feel land – some land – must be near: It might not be Ireland, but any land would do just then.

Bill, of course, was at the controls. Slim, gnawing a sandwich, sat beside him, when out of the mists there grew a blue shadow, in appearance no more solid than hundreds of other nebulous 'landscapes' we had sighted before. For a while Slim studied it, then turned and called Bill's attention to it.

It was land!

20HRS, 40 MIN … Our Flight in the Friendship, Amelia Earhart

Understanding the autobiography

- Where did the flight take off from?
- What was:
  a the intended destination   b the actual destination?
- What was the name of the aeroplane?
- How long did the flight take?
- What were the two main problems towards the end of the flight?

Looking at words

Explain the meaning of these words and phrases as they are used in the extract.

a bearing   b log   c perplexed
d keep faith   e epitomised   f holding true
g fuselage   h altitude   i nebulous

Exploring further

- What do you think the *America* was?
- When Bill dropped the notes, what was he trying to find out?
- Explain, in your own words, why they had 'no luck' with the notes.
- Reread the paragraph beginning, 'We could see only a few miles of water …'.
  How do you think they were feeling:
  a before they saw the fishing vessel   b after they saw the fishing vessel?
- What impression do you get of Amelia Earhart?

Extra

The flight across the Atlantic is 2,246 miles. Look at the photograph of Amelia Earhart and her plane.

- Why do you think she went on such a dangerous journey?
- Would you have done it or not? Explain your reasons.

TEACH continued ...

- Find an example where Shackleton:
  - records a fact
    For example, 'built there by the Swedish expedition in 1902'.
  - expresses a feeling.
    For example, 'hope beat high'.
- What impression do you get of Shackleton?
  Answers suggesting that he was courageous / practical / cared about his crew / was deeply affected by the loss of his ship.
- Does the extract convey the awful situation Shackleton and his men find themselves in? Explain your reasons.
  Answers that suggest the extract does give a good impression of what they were going through but that it is not over-dramatic. Shackleton explains what is happening in a calm, detailed way, but the reader does understand how the loss of the ship affected him.

Plenary

- Ask pupils to imagine they were one of the sailors on the *Endurance* and they now face a 364-mile walk across the ice to find shelter. How would they be feeling? What would their attitude be to Shackleton?

TALK

Before reading

- What do pupils know about the history of flight?

- Can they tell you anything about the Wright brothers?
- What did the very first planes look like?

Reading

- Explain to pupils that they are going to read an extract from an autobiography called *20 HRS, 40 MIN ... Our Flight in the Friendship* by Amelia Earhart, the first woman to fly across the Atlantic.
- Background information: Amelia Earhart was born in America in 1898. She was the first woman to fly accompanied across the Atlantic Ocean, to fly solo across it (1932) and the Pacific Ocean (1935). Her plane was lost over the Pacific Ocean on an attempted flight around the world in 1937.
- The extract can be read to the class by the teacher, by individuals in the class or as a group.

Discussion group

In groups, pupils discuss the questions and make notes on their responses. Ensure pupils understand that they do not always have to agree.

Understanding the autobiography

- Where did the flight take off from?
  It took off from Trespassy in Canada.
- What was:
  a the intended destination?
  The intended destination was Ireland;
  b the actual destination?
  The actual destination was Burry Port.

- What was the name of the aeroplane?
  The name of the aeroplane was Friendship.
- How long did the flight take?
  The flight took 20 hours and 40 minutes.
- What were the two main problems towards the end of the flight?
  '... we had but one hour's supply of gas left' / '... our radio was useless.'

Looking at words

Explain the meaning of these words and phrases as they are used in the extract:
a bearing: *position;* **b log:** *written record of the flight;* **c perplexed:** *puzzled;* **d keep faith:** *stick to;* **e epitomised:** *the perfect word for;* **f holding true:** *on the right course;* **g fuselage:** *the body of an aeroplane;* **h altitude:** *height;* **i nebulous:** *cloud-like.*

Exploring further

- What do you think the *America* was?
  Answers suggesting it was some sort of ship.
- When Bill dropped the notes, what was he trying to find out?
  Answers suggesting he was trying to find out where they were, i.e. how close to land.
- Explain, in your own words, why they had 'no luck' with the notes.
  Using evidence from the text, answers suggesting that the combination of 'our speed' (they were going too fast), 'the movement of the vessel' (the ship wasn't still – it was also moving), 'the wind' (carrying the bag off course) and 'the lightness of the missile' (it wasn't heavy enough to drop straight down) meant that they had 'no luck' with the notes.

Touching the Void

In June 1985, Joe Simpson and Simon Yates climbed 21,000 ft to the top of Siula Grande in the Andes. On the way down, disaster struck! Joe's ice hammer came out of the mountain wall and …

… there was a sharp cracking sound and my right hand, gripping the axe, pulled down. The sudden jerk turned me outwards and instantly I was falling.

I hit the slope at the base of the cliff before I saw it coming. I was facing into the slope and both knees locked as I struck it. I felt a shattering blow in my knee, felt bones splitting, and screamed. The impact catapulted me over backwards and down the slope of the East Face. I slid, head-first, on my back. The rushing speed of it confused me. I thought of the drop below but felt nothing. Simon would be ripped off the mountain. He couldn't hold this. I screamed again as I jerked to a sudden violent stop.

Everything was still, silent. My thoughts raced madly. Then pain flooded down my thigh – a fierce burning fire coming down the inside of my thigh, seeming to ball in my groin, building and building until I cried out at it, and my breathing came in ragged gasps. My leg! Oh Jesus. My leg!

I hung, head down, on my back, left leg tangled in the rope above me, and my right leg hanging slackly to one side. I lifted my head from the snow and stared, up across my chest, at a grotesque distortion in the right knee, twisting the leg into a strange zigzag. I didn't connect it with the pain which burnt in my groin. That had nothing to do with my knee. I kicked my left leg free of the rope and swung round until I was hanging against the snow on my chest, feet down. The pain eased. I kicked my left foot into the slope and stood up.

A wave of nausea surged over me. I pressed my face into the snow, and the sharp cold seemed to calm me. Something terrible, something dark with dread occurred to me, and as I thought about it I felt the dark thought break into panic: 'I've broken my leg, that's it. I'm dead. Everyone said it … if there's just two of you a broken ankle could turn into a death sentence … if it's broken … if …' It doesn't hurt so much, maybe I've just ripped something.

I kicked my right leg against the slope, feeling sure it wasn't broken. My knee exploded. Bone grated, and the fireball rushed from groin to knee. I screamed. I looked down at the knee and could see it was broken, yet I tried not to believe what I was seeing. It wasn't just broken, it was ruptured, twisted, crushed, and I could see the kink in the joint and knew what had happened. The impact had driven my lower leg up through the knee joint.

Touching the Void, Joe Simpson

Understanding the autobiography

1 Name the two men climbing in the Andes.
2 Which mountain were they climbing?
3 Which side of the mountain were they on?
4 What could a minor injury, such as a broken ankle, mean for only two climbers on a mountain?

Understanding the words

5 Explain the meaning of these words and phrases as they are used in the extract.

  a locked   b catapulted   c grotesque distortion

  d nausea   e ruptured   f impact

Exploring further

6 What do you think Joe means when he says, 'Simon would be ripped off the mountain. He couldn't hold this'?
7 Joe says, 'My thoughts raced madly'. What 'thoughts' do you think were going through his mind at this point?
8 Explain, in your own words, what the 'something dark with dread' was that occurred to Joe.
9 Joe's right leg was injured. Why do you think he kicked it 'against the slope'?
10 What impression do you get of Joe Simpson?

Extra

Simon was above Joe on the mountain. He couldn't see what had happened but he knew something was wrong.

Imagine you are Simon and write briefly about the incident from your point of view. Remember that as well as the facts, you need to include your thoughts and feelings.

work (*Teach*) and group work (*Talk*) about the common features of autobiographical writing.

Round-up

- Use pupils' answers to the 'Extra' activity as the basis for a class discussion.
- How do pupils know that Joe did not die on the mountain?
- Recap on what pupils have learnt about autobiographical writing. (First person, past tense, facts, feelings.)

Reading

- Explain to pupils that they are going to read an extract from an autobiography called *Touching the Void*, an incredible story of courage and survival.
- The extract can be read to the class by the teacher, by individuals in the class or individually.

Questions

Pupils answer the questions individually, drawing on what they have learnt from previous class

---

ICT

TALK continued ...

- Reread the paragraph beginning, '*We could see only a few miles of water ...*'. How do you think they were feeling:

  a before they saw the fishing vessel?

  Answers suggesting they felt quite desperate. They could see very little in cloud, could not make radio contact and were running out of fuel.

  b after they saw the fishing vessel?

  Answers suggesting they felt relieved because this meant they were near land.

- What impression do you get of Amelia Earhart?

  Answers suggesting she was courageous / adventurous / loved flying.

Extra

Ensure all members of the group contribute opinions. One pupil should make notes on the discussion.

Plenary

Use pupils' answers to the 'Extra' activity as the basis for a class discussion.

WRITE

Before reading

- Discuss what pupils think about mountain climbing. Can they see the appeal?
- What sort of people do they think go mountain climbing?
- Would they like to? Why? Why not?

ICT

? Answer guidance

Understanding the autobiography

1 Joe Simpson and Simon Yates.
2 They were climbing Siula Grande.
3 They were on the East Face.
4 A minor injury could mean 'a death sentence'.

Understanding the words

5 **a** *locked*: became rigidly immovable;
  b *catapulted*: threw;
  c *grotesque distortion*: unnaturally out of shape;
  d *nausea*: sickness;
  e *ruptured*: burst;
  f *impact*: force (with which he kicked the slope).

Thinking about facts and opinions

6 Answers suggesting that Simon is on the other end of the rope and, when Joe falls, he will find it almost impossible not to fall after him.

---

7 Answers suggesting that he thought about what had happened / Simon / how he was injured / how he could get back on the mountain, etc.
8 Answers suggesting that what occurred to Joe was the thought that he might die.
9 Answers suggesting that Joe would not accept that he had injured his leg because it would probably mean certain death. He wanted to prove to himself that his leg was all right.
10 Answers suggesting that he was courageous / he didn't give up but tried to help himself / even in that difficult situation he was unselfish enough to think about what might happen to Simon.

Extra

Individual answers.

The Tower of London
▶ Understanding the conventions of
formal writing

The Tower of London

History of the Tower of London

William the Conqueror (1035–1087) built the Tower of London for the purpose of protecting the city. **Tradition** has it that it was started in 1078 and took 20 years to complete. The White Tower was the first stone keep to be built in Britain and is the only part left of the original building. Large quantities of stone were **transported** to the site to build the huge walls that extended 33.5 metres east/west, 36.5 metres north/south, and were 27.5 metres high. Over the centuries, the buildings on the site have been extended and now, including the moat, cover 18 acres.

In the reign of Henry III (1216–1272) the Tower was extended and enclosed by a new **curtain wall**. Edward I (1272–1307) continued improving the castle's defences by having two curtain walls, one inside the other. The inner wall was higher so the outer wall could be defended from it.

Throughout its history, the Tower of London has been **fortress**, palace and prison; the home of the Royal Mint and the Royal Observatory; housed a large **arsenal** of small arms and the Crown Jewels. From the 13th century onwards it was also the home of the Royal Menagerie that evolved into London Zoo.

46

Up until as late as the 17th century, control of the Tower of London was essential to control of London itself. The Tower was a stronghold from which London could be defended, but it was also a **refuge** for when the **monarch** was in danger. Safe within its walls, a monarch could organise his supporters or come to some agreement with the enemy – an enemy that was often the people of London, who were less than pleased with their monarch's actions.

The Tower of London became one of many royal houses. In many reigns it was hardly used at all, but almost every monarch stayed there before his or her **coronation**. After spending the night at the Tower, the monarch-to-be would ride in a great procession through the streets of London to Westminster Abbey to be crowned. This procession was to please the people of London whose support was so important to a successful reign. The last of these processions from the Tower to the Abbey was made by Charles II in 1661.

Although no monarch has actually lived in the Tower of London for over 400 years, it still has the title of a royal palace.

- For what purpose was the Tower of London built?
- How many does the site now cover?
- When did almost every monarch stay at the Tower of London?
- Where are the kings and queens of England crowned?
- Explain the meaning of the words and phrases in **bold**.
- What do you understand by the phrase 'tradition has it'?
- What do you think was the purpose of:
  - the Royal Mint
  - the Royal Observatory?
- Why do you think the monarch had to please the people of London?
- How has the writer organised the information about the Tower of London?
- Do you think the photographs help the reader to understand the text? Why? Why not?
- This is the introduction to a guidebook about the Tower of London. Do you think it is useful or not? Explain your reasons.

Extracts

The Tower of London
A Guide to the Tower of London
Spectres of the Past

Planning

Formal writing

Objectives

Renewed Primary Literacy Framework Year 6

1 Speaking
• Use talk to explore ideas, topics or issues.

2 Listening and responding
• Identify the ways spoken language varies according to the differences in context and purpose.

7 Understanding and interpreting text
• Understanding how writers use different structures to create coherence.

Assessment focuses

AF2 Understand, describe, select or retrieve information, events or ideas from texts and use quotation and reference to text
L3–L5 Increasingly and clearly identifies relevant points from across a text and supports them by reference to the text.
AF5 Explain and comment on writers' use of language, including grammatical and literary features
L3/L4/L5 Identifies increasing number of features of writer's language and its effects.

Scottish Curriculum for Excellence: Literacy
Listening and Talking
Understanding, analysing, evaluating (third level)
Can recognise the difference between fact and opinion.
Reading
Finding and using information (third / fourth levels)
Using knowledge of features of text types, can find, select and sort information and use this for different purposes.

TEACH

In this unit pupils are given the opportunity to investigate formal writing through three extracts for a guidebook about the Tower of London, giving a brief history of the Tower, a guided tour of the most famous parts, and details of the supposed hauntings that occur within its walls.

Before reading

• What do pupils know about the Tower of London?

• Have they ever visited the Tower?

• Why do they think it is a popular place for tourists to visit?

Reading

• Explain to the pupils that they are going to read the introduction to a guidebook on the Tower of London where a brief history is given.

• The extract can be read to the class by the teacher, aloud by individual children in turn, or in silence individually.

After reading

Use the panel prompts in the Pupil Book as the basis of a class discussion.

• For what purpose was the Tower of London built?
Its purpose was 'protecting the city'.

• How many acres does the site now cover?
It covers 18 acres.

• When did 'almost every monarch' stay at the Tower of London?
A monarch stayed at the Tower 'before his or her coronation'.

• Where are the kings and queens of England crowned?
They are crowned at Westminster Abbey.

• Explain the meaning of the words and phrases in bold.
tradition: what has always been said; transported: carried; curtain wall: a wall connecting two towers; fortress: military stronghold; arsenal: store of weapons; refuge: place of safety; monarch: ruler (king or queen); coronation: crowning of a king or queen.

• What do you understand by the phrase 'Tradition has it'?
Answers suggesting that while it is thought that the Tower was started in 1078, there is no actual proof.

• What do you think was the purpose of:
  • the Royal Mint?
  to make coins (money);
  • the Royal Observatory?
  for scientific study, especially astronomy.

• Why do you think the monarch had 'to please the people of London'?
Answers based on evidence: '... an enemy that was often the people of London – the monarch needed to keep the people on his / her side to prevent them turning against him / her.

• How has the writer organised the information about the Tower of London?
Answers suggesting that it is organised chronologically, from the Tower being built through to the present day.

ICT

A GUIDE TO

THE TOWER OF LONDON

One of Britain's most popular tourist attractions with several million visitors each year. This is a guide to the most famous parts of the Tower that should not be missed.

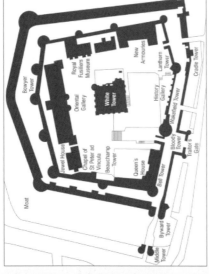

The Armouries

Housed in the White Tower, armour and weapons from the Middle Ages onward are displayed in the Armouries. The earliest examples are of chain mail for the body and legs. A helmet was worn and extra protection given by a shield carried on the left arm. Weapons were the lance and the sword and, to a lesser degree, the mace and the axe. As well as weapons and armour used for sport, tournaments and combat, one can also see an example of an execution block and axe. Oriental weapons are on display in the New Armouries to the east of the White Tower.

The Wakefield Tower

Probably named after William de Wakefield, a senior court official in the reign of Edward III, it is most famous for being the scene of Anne Boleyn's trial. The second wife of Henry VIII failed to produce a male heir. Charges of treason were brought against her and she was executed in 1536.

The Bloody Tower

Formerly known as the Garden Tower, it was given its gruesome name because of the deaths of 'the Princes in the Tower'. Edward V (12) and his brother, the Duke of York (10), are thought to have been murdered by the Duke of Gloucester on his way to becoming King Richard III.

The Jewel House

Most of the jewels on display date from the 17th century as many of the earlier ones were melted down by Oliver Cromwell. The oldest crown to be seen was made for the coronation of Charles II. Other items, such as Queen Victoria's Imperial State Crown, sceptre, orbs and swords, can be seen in the Jewel House.

Traitor's Gate

Traitor's Gate is situated below St Thomas's Tower. It was originally a main entrance via the Thames. In later years it was used to bring prisoners to the Tower after they had been tried and convicted at Westminster. Such famous prisoners as Anne Boleyn, Sir Thomas More and Thomas Cromwell passed through these gates on the way to imprisonment or execution.

Understanding the guide

- Why is it thought the name of the Garden Tower was changed?
- What is the Wakefield Tower most famous for?
- Who wore the Imperial State Crown at her coronation?
- Where were people tried before being imprisoned in the Tower?

Looking at words

Explain the meaning of these words and phrases as they are used in the guide.

a to a lesser degree	b mace	c combat
d sceptre	e orbs	f male heir
g treason	h Formerly known as	i gruesome

Exploring further

- How do you think the writer of the guide worked out which are the 'most popular' parts of the Tower?
- Why do you think the Duke of Gloucester may have murdered the princes?
- Do you think Charles II ruled England before or after Oliver Cromwell? Explain your reasons.
- Why do you think 'Traitor's Gate' is so called?
- Why do you think the writer has included a plan of the Tower of London?

Extra

Using the plan of the Tower, work out a circular route so that a visitor sees everything mentioned in the guide.

a to a lesser degree: *not used as much;* **b mace:** *heavy club;* **c combat:** *fighting;* **d sceptre:** *royal staff;* **e orbs:** *globes, each with a cross on top;* **f male heir:** *son;* **g treason:** *crimes against the monarch;* **h formerly known as:** *was previously called;* **i gruesome:** *horrible / disgusting.*

Exploring further

● How do you think the writer of the guide worked out which are the most popular parts of the Tower?
Answers that suggest the writer researched visitor numbers / spoke to people who work at the Tower.

● Why do you think the Duke of Gloucester may have murdered the princes?
Answers suggesting that as 'Princes' they were next in line to the throne and the Duke of Gloucester wanted them out of way so he could be king.

● Do you think Charles II ruled England before or after Oliver Cromwell? Explain your reasons.
Answers suggesting that Charles II ruled after Oliver Cromwell as Cromwell had melted down many of the earlier jewels but we can still see this one.

● Why do you think 'Traitor's Gate' is so called?
Answers suggesting it is called this because prisoners convicted of being traitors entered the Tower through this gate.

● Why do you think the writer has included a plan of the Tower of London?
Answers that suggest the plan shows you where these places are and how you can get to them.

Extra

Ensure all members of the group contribute. One pupil can make notes of the discussion.

Reading

● Explain to the pupils that they are going to read another extract from the guidebook to the Tower of London, this time giving information about the places in the Tower that should not be missed.

● The extract can be read to the class by the teacher, by individuals in the class or as a group.

Discussion group

In groups, pupils discuss the questions and make notes on their responses. Ensure pupils understand that they do not always have to agree.

Understanding the guide

● Why is it thought the name of the Garden Tower was changed?
The name was changed 'because of the deaths of the Princes in the Tower'.

● What is the Wakefield Tower most famous for?
It is famous 'for being the scene of Anne Boleyn's trial'.

● Who wore the Imperial State Crown at her coronation?
Queen Victoria wore the crown.

● Where were people tried before being imprisoned in the Tower?
They were tried at Westminster.

Looking at words

● Explain the meaning of these words and phrases as they are used in the guide:

TEACH continued ...

● Do you think the photographs help the reader to understand the text? Why? Why not?
Answers suggesting the photographs help as they show what is being written about.

● This is the introduction to a guidebook about the Tower of London. Do you think it is useful or not? Explain your reasons.
Individual answers.

Plenary

● Use the plenary session to tackle the concept of formal writing. Pupils are often clearer about what is required when examples of what is *not* appropriate are given.

● Pick out words and phrases and 'translate' them into informal language and ask pupils to comment, for example: *monarch – the bloke in charge; prison – nick.*

● Why is it appropriate to use standard English in a guidebook?

TALK

Before reading

● In most places you visit, you can buy a book that tells you what you are looking at. Ask pupils why they think this is called a 'guidebook'?

● As well as the history, what else do pupils think they will find in a guidebook for the Tower of London?

73

Spectres of the Past

During the Tower of London's 900-year history, it has become known as one of the most haunted places in Britain.

The first reported sighting

Thomas Becket was the Archbishop of Canterbury in the reign of Henry II. He quarrelled with the king and was murdered in Canterbury Cathedral on Henry's orders. When Henry III, Henry II's grandson, was building a curtain wall at the Tower of London, the story goes that the ghost of Thomas Becket appeared and struck the wall with his cross, reducing it to rubble. Henry III lost no time in naming a tower after Becket to appease his ghost, which was never seen again.

The princes in the Tower

Tradition says that the princes were locked up in the Bloody Tower and put to death on the orders of the future king, Richard III. In the late 15th century, guards passing the Bloody Tower reported two small figures gliding down the stairs. They wore the nightshirts the princes had on when they disappeared. They stood hand in hand before they seemed to fade back into the wall.

The most persistent haunting

The ghost that appears more than any other is that of Anne Boleyn. Accounts persist that she appears near the Queen's House, close to the site of her execution. Her headless body has also been sighted walking the corridors of the Tower.

A gruesome execution

The Countess of Salisbury was put to death by order of King Henry VIII. She would not put her head on the block and ran from her executioner. He pursued her, attacking her with the axe until she was dead. Some say they have seen her ghost re-enacting her death and the shadow of the axe hanging over the scene of her murder.

The Salt Tower

This is one of the most haunted areas of the Tower of London. Some say dogs will not enter the Salt Tower since a guard was nearly strangled by an unseen force. In 1864 a soldier guarding the Queen's House challenged what he thought was an intruder. Getting no reply he charged with his bayonet and went straight through the apparition.

Understanding the guide

1 How old is the Tower of London?
2 Who saw the ghosts of the two princes?
3 Which ghost appears more than any other?
4 Which is the most haunted area of the Tower?

Understanding the words

5 Explain the meaning of these words and phrases as they are used in the guide.

a the story goes   b appease   c future king   d persist
e pursued   f re-enacting   g bayonet   h apparition

Exploring further

6 What evidence is there in the guide to show that Henry III probably believed in ghosts?
7 What do you understand about the story of the princes in the Tower from the phrase 'Tradition says'?
8 Why do you think the ghost of Anne Boleyn appears 'headless'?
9 What do most of these ghosts have in common?
10 Why do you think the writer has included these ghost stories in the guide?

Extra

Has the guide to the Tower of London made you want to visit it or not? Explain your reasons.

TALK *continued …*

Plenary

- Use pupils' answers to the 'Extra' activity as the basis for a class discussion.

- Revisit the extract using the same technique as for the first extract in the unit, that is, by selecting words and phrases to translate into informal language, for example: *imprisonment – being banged up*; *execution – getting the chop*, etc.

WRITE

Before reading

- What do pupils understand by the term 'spectre'?

- Would they be interested in seeing places that are supposed to be haunted? Why? Why not?

Reading

- Explain to pupils that they are going to read a third extract, called 'Spectres of the Past', from the guidebook, which deals with the ghostly goings-on at the Tower of London.

- The extract can be read to the class by the teacher, by individuals in the class or individually.

Questions

Pupils answer the questions individually, drawing on what they have learnt from previous class work (*Teach*) and group work (*Talk*) about the conventions of formal writing.

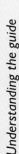 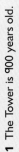

? Answer guidance

Understanding the guide

1 The Tower is 900 years old.
2 The ghosts were seen by 'guards passing the Bloody Tower'.
3 The ghost of Anne Boleyn.
4 The Salt Tower.

Understanding the words

5 a *the story goes*: these are the details of the story, but there is no proof;
  b *appease*: satisfy / calm / make amends;
  c *future king*: not king at the time;
  d *persist*: continue, going on and on;
  e *pursued*: chased;
  f *re-enacting*: doing it again;
  g *bayonet*: stabbing blade attached to a rifle;
  h *apparition*: ghost/spectre.

ICT

Exploring further

6 Answers based on evidence: 'Henry III lost no time in naming a tower after Becket to appease his ghost …'.
7 Answers that suggest the story is what people have always believed but that there is no actual proof.
8 Answers that suggest she met her death by being beheaded.
9 Answers based on evidence that they were murdered / executed.
10 Answers that suggest such stories are popular and will be of interest to the tourists.

Extra

Individual answers. Look for children drawing on references from the text, and identifying other things they wish to find out.

Round-up

- Use pupils' answers to the 'Extra' activity as the basis for a class discussion.

- Review with them what they understand by 'formal writing'.

Unit 9

Danger at sea!
▶ Understanding an author's themes and techniques

Why the Whales Came

'As long as we keep Scilly Rock **astern** of us we can pull home easily enough,' Daniel said softly.

'But how are we going to do that if we can't see it?' I whispered, taking the oar he was handing me. 'I can't see it anymore.'

'We can hear it though, can't we?' he said. 'Listen.' And certainly I could hear the surge of the sea **seething** around Scilly Rock as it always did even on the calmest of days. 'Hear it?' he said. 'Just keep that sound astern of us and we'll be able to feel our way home. Gweal must be dead ahead from here. There's no **swell** to speak of, so we won't go on the rocks. All we have to do is **to hug the coast** all the way round and that'll bring us nicely into Popplestones.'

And so we began to row, only a few strokes at a time, stopping to listen for the sea around Scilly Rock. It was not long though before I began to think that Gweal was not at all where it should have been. We had already been rowing quite long enough and hard enough to have reached it by now. Then I thought that, perhaps the current must have dragged us off course, that we must be somewhere between Samson and Bryher, that I could still hear Scilly Rock somewhere astern of us and distant, but Daniel was no longer even sure of that. We pulled until our arms could pull no longer, but still no land **loomed** up out of the fog as we expected. Within half an hour we had to admit to each other that we were quite lost. We sat over our oars and drifted, straining our ears for the wash of the sea against the rocks, anything to give us some idea of where we were. The fog though seemed to **obscure** and shroud the sounds of the sea just as it was hiding the islands that we knew lay all around us. Even the piping of invisible oystercatchers was dulled and deadened as the dark came down through the fog and settled around us.

Strange as it may seem, the darkness came as a kind of comfort to us, for at least it was the kind of blindness we were accustomed to. Even Daniel who was never fond of the dark seemed relieved at the **onset** of night. We searched now for some crack in the blackness about us, a glimmer of a light from the shore that would guide us safely home. We sat beside each other huddled together and silent, the damp jibsail wrapped around us to keep out the cold, peering constantly into the **impenetrable** night and listening, always listening for the hiss of surf on the shingle or the distant **muted** charge of the waves against the cliffs.

Often during that long, long night our hopes were raised by the whisper

of waves on some far shore, and we would row frantically towards it for a few minutes and then sit silent and listen again, only to discover it had been nothing but wishful thinking, a trick of the mind. Either it was that or we had simply been rowing the wrong way – we could never be sure which. In this dense darkness all sense of direction, time and space seemed to be **distorted**. Each time our hopes were raised only to be dashed, and each time the disappointment was all the more cruel and all the more lasting.

The cold had numbed my feet up to my knees and my hands could no longer feel the oar I was pulling. I wanted so much just to go to sleep, to give up and go to sleep. But Daniel would not let me.

Why the Whales Came, Michael Morpurgo

- What is the setting for this part of the story?
- At the beginning of the extract, why can't the characters see Scilly Rock?
- What does Daniel say they can use to find their way home?
- How is the narrator feeling at the end of the extract?
- Explain the meaning of the words and phrases in **bold**.
- Explain, in your own words, why the narrator says, 'the darkness came as a kind of comfort to us.'
- What does the narrator mean when she says that 'the whisper of waves on some far shore' was only 'wishful thinking'?
- Why do you think Daniel would not let the narrator go to sleep?
- When you read this extract, how does the writer want you to feel?

Extracts

Why the Whales Came Michael Morpurgo
The Ghost of Grania O'Malley Michael Morpurgo
Kensuke's Kingdom Michael Morpurgo

Planning

Authors and texts

Objectives

Renewed Primary Literacy Framework Year 6
1 Speaking
• Use talk to explore ideas, topics or issues.
4 Drama
• Improvise using a range of drama strategies and conventions to explore themes.
7 Understanding and interpreting texts
• Understand underlying themes, causes and points of view.

Assessment focuses
AF3 Deduce, infer or interpret information, events or ideas from texts
L3–L5 Increasingly makes inferences and deductions based on evidence across a text.
AF5 Explain and comment on writers' use of language, including grammatical and literary features
L3/L4/L5 Shows increasing awareness of features of writer's language and comments on effects of these.

Scottish Curriculum for Excellence: Literacy
Listening and Talking
Understanding, analysing, evaluating (second / third levels)
Responds to literal, inferential, evaluative and other types of questions; asks different kinds of questions; comments with evidence on content and form of short texts.
Reading
Understanding, analysing, evaluating (third / fourth levels)
Shows understanding across different areas of learning, identifies and considers the purpose and main ideas of a text and uses supporting detail; makes inferences from key statements.

TEACH

In this unit pupils are given the opportunity to investigate the work of one author, Michael Morpurgo. For the purposes of allowing pupils to identify common themes, the extracts chosen have child characters and the sea as a link but the diversity of the author's work should be made clear to pupils and they should be encouraged to read his books.

Before reading
• Discuss the pupils' favourite authors.
• Discuss Michael Morpurgo with the pupils, and any of his books they have read, for example, *Private Peaceful* and *Kensuke's Kingdom*.

Reading
• Explain to the pupils that they are going to read an extract from *Why the Whales Came.*
• The story so far: Gracie and Daniel are friends and live in the Scilly Isles. When the men go off to war, times are hard. Gracie's mother works hard but is always short of money. Gracie and Daniel decide to go fishing, hoping to catch enough fish for her mother to sell – and that's when they get into difficulties.
• The extract can be read to the class by the teacher, aloud by individual children in turn, or in silence individually.

After reading
Use the panel prompts in the Pupil Book as the basis of a class discussion.

ICT

• What is the setting for this part of the story?
The setting is a boat on the sea.

• At the beginning of the extract, why can't the characters see Scilly Rock?
They could not see because of the fog.

• What does Daniel say they can use to find their way home?
He says they can use their hearing – 'the surge of the sea seething around Scilly Rock'.

• How is the narrator feeling at the end of the extract?
'The cold had numbed my feet up to my knees and my hands could no longer feel the oar I was pulling. I wanted so much just to go to sleep, to give up …'

• Explain the meaning of the words and phrases in bold.
astern: to the back of the boat; seething: bubbling in a very agitated manner; swell: heaving of the sea with waves that do not break; to lug the coast: (to row the boat) following the coastline; loomed: appeared out of; obscure: deaden; onset: start; impenetrable: cannot be seen through / into; muted: muffled; distorted: changed.

• Explain, in your own words, why the narrator says, 'the darkness came as a kind of comfort to us'.
Answers that suggest they were used to not being able to see in the darkness, and the more dark it got, the more chance they would have of seeing a light from the land.

• What does the narrator mean when she says that 'the whisper of waves on some far shore' was only 'wishful thinking'?
Answers that suggest they wanted to hear the waves around Scilly Rock so badly that they made themselves believe they could.

Lost at Sea

Jessie Parsons lives on Clare Island. Her American cousin, Jack, comes to stay with her for the summer. Jessie's father takes them fishing but has to return home when his rod breaks, leaving the children on the rocks. Then disaster strikes!

That was the moment the fish caught on and Jack shouted, 'I've got one! I've got one!' He braced his legs and began to reel in furiously. Then he slipped. His legs went from under him and he was sliding past her towards the edge.

Instinctively, Jessie reached out for him. For a fleeting moment she had hold of his jeans, just long enough for Jack to cling on to a rock and stop his slide. But then Jessie herself was slipping, rolling over and over and over, trying to find something to clutch at, anything. But there was nothing, no way she could stop herself. She caught a glimpse of Jack throwing himself full-stretch on the rock to save her. Then she was over the edge and falling through the air. The sea smothered her before she could scream. The water came into her mouth and into her ears and she was sinking deeper and deeper and could do nothing about it.

She looked up. There was light up above her, light she knew she had to reach if she was to live, but her legs wouldn't kick and her flailing arms seemed incapable of helping her. She had often thought about how drowning would be, when she was out in her father's boat or crossing over from the mainland on the ferry. And now she was drowning. This was how it was. Her eyes were stinging, so she closed them. She closed her mouth too, so she wouldn't swallow any more seawater. But she had to breathe – she couldn't help herself. She gasped and the seawater came in again and she began to choke.

Then something was holding her down. She fought, but the grip tightened about her waist and would not let go. Her head broke water, and suddenly there was air, wonderful air to breathe. She was spluttering and coughing. Someone was shouting at her. It was Jack and he was holding her. 'It's me! It's me! Hang on, just hang on to me. You'll be OK.' His face was near hers. 'Can you swim?' She shook her head. 'Just try to keep your mouth closed. Someone'll see us. We'll be OK. We'll be fine.'

Jessie looked beyond him. The shore was already a long way off and they were being carried away from it all the time. She looked the other way. Whenever they came up to the top of a wave she could see the bank of mist rolling over the sea towards them. One more wave and the mist would swallow them and then no one would ever see them.

'We've got to keep floating,' Jack cried. 'Just hang on.' 'The cold had numbed her legs already and she knew her arms couldn't hold on much longer. And then the mist came over their heads and shrouded them completely. Jack was crying out for help, screaming. She tried herself, but could only manage a whimper. It was hopeless.

The Ghost of Grania O'Malley, Michael Morpurgo

Understanding the extract

- What are the two settings for this extract?
- What caused Jack to slip?
- What was Jessie trying to do when she slipped?
- What happened before she could scream?
- What did Jack say they had to keep doing?

Looking at words

Explain the meaning of these words and phrases as they are used in the extract.

a furiously   b Instinctively   c fleeting moment

d flailing   e shrouded   f whimper

Exploring further

- What do you think was going through Jessie's mind as she was falling?
- Why do you think she 'fought' when Jack was trying to rescue her?
- Do you think Jack believed what he was saying when he said, 'We'll be fine'? Explain your reasons.
- Explain, in your own words, why Jessie did not believe him.
- How do you think Jack felt when:

  a he saw Jessie going into the water

  b he dived in to save her

  c he was 'crying out for help'?

Extra

What do you think Jack and Jessie can do to save themselves?

● Why do you think Daniel would not let the narrator go to sleep?
Answers that suggest it is dangerous to go to sleep when you are really cold.

● When you read this extract, how does the writer want you to feel?
Individual answers based on evidence from the text: use of the first person describing her feelings helps the reader empathise and imagine the narrator's desperate situation.

Plenary

If the pupils know the story, can they relate what happens? If they don't know the story, can they predict what might happen?

TALK

Before reading

● Recap on the main features of the previous extract: characters live on an island / sail boats / get into difficulty.

Reading

● Explain to pupils that they are going to read an extract from *The Ghost of Grania O'Malley* where, again, the sea plays an important part.

● The extract can be read to the class by the teacher, by individuals in the class or as a group.

Discussion group

In groups, pupils discuss the questions and make notes on their responses. Ensure pupils understand that they do not always have to agree.

Understanding the extract

● What are the two settings for this extract?
The settings are the rocks and the sea.

● What caused Jack to slip?
He caught a fish and was reeling it in.

● What was Jessie trying to do when she slipped?
'Jessie reached out for him.'

● What happened before she could scream?
'The sea smothered her before she could scream.'

● What did Jack say they had to keep doing?
'We've got to keep floating.'

Looking at words

Explain the meaning of these words and phrases as they are used in the extract:

a **furiously:** *very quickly / with great energy;*
b **instinctively:** *without thinking;* c **fleeting moment:** *a split second;* d **flailing:** *swinging wildly about;*
e **shrouded:** *hid;* f **whimper:** *a feeble, frightened sound.*

Exploring further

● What do you think was going through Jessie's mind as she was falling?
Answers that suggest she was frightened because she tried to scream.

● Why do you think she 'fought' when Jack was trying to rescue her?

Answers that suggest she did not know what was happening. All she could feel was 'something holding her down'.

● Do you think Jack believed what he was saying when he said, 'We'll be fine'? Explain your reasons.

Answers that suggest he did not really believe what he was saying but rather he was trying to calm Jessie down so he could hold on to her.

● Explain, in your own words, why Jessie did not believe him.

Answers based on evidence: 'The shore was already a long way off' / 'they were being carried away from it' / 'she could see the bank of mist rolling over the sea towards them' / 'the mist would swallow them and then no one would ever see them'.

● How do you think Jack felt when:
a he saw Jessie go into the water?
shocked / fearful;

b he dived in to save her?
he knew he had to do it / probably acted instinctively;

c he was 'crying out for help'?
very scared / desperate.

Extra

Ensure all members of the group contribute ideas. One pupil should make notes of the discussion.

Plenary

Use pupils' answers for the 'Extra' activity as the basis for a class discussion. What are the similarities and differences between the two extracts?

Alone in the Ocean

*Michael's parents are both made redundant. His father decides to buy a boat called
the Peggy Sue. So Michael, his mum and dad, and their dog Stella, set off to sail
round the world. One night his parents are sleeping and Michael is in charge of the
boat. Stella is barking and she hasn't got her safety harness on …*

… So I left the wheel and went forward to bring her back. I took the ball
with me to sweeten her in, to tempt her away from the bow of the boat.

I crouched down. 'Come on, Stella,' I said, rolling the ball from hand
to hand. I knew then I shouldn't have left the wheel. The ball rolled away
from me quite suddenly. I lunged after it, but it was gone over the
side before I could grab it. I lay there on the deck watching it
bob away into the darkness. I was furious with myself for being
so silly.

I was still cursing myself when I thought I heard the
sound of singing. Someone was singing out there in the
darkness. I called but no one replied. So that was what
Stella had been barking at.

I looked again for my ball, but by now it had
disappeared. That ball had been very precious to me,
precious to all of us. I knew I had just lost a great deal more
than a football.

I was angry with Stella. The whole thing had been her
fault. She was still barking. I couldn't hear the singing
anymore. I called her again, whistled her in. She wouldn't
come. I got to my feet and went forward. I took her by the
collar and pulled. She would not be moved. I couldn't drag
her all the way back, so I bent down to pick her up. She
was still reluctant. Then I had her in my arms, but she was
struggling.

I heard the wind above me in the sail. I remember
thinking: this is silly, you haven't got your safety harness
on, you haven't got your lifejacket on, you shouldn't be
doing this. Then the boat veered violently and I was thrown
sideways. With my arms full I had no time to grab the guard
rail. We were in the cold of the sea before I could even open
my mouth to scream.

The terrors came fast, one upon another: The
lights of the Peggy Sue went away in the dark of the
night, leaving me alone in the ocean, alone with the
certainty that they were already too far away, that my
cries for help could not possibly be heard. I thought
then of sharks cruising the black water beneath me
– scenting me, already searching me out, homing in
on me – and I knew there could be no hope. I would
be eaten alive. Either that or I would drown slowly.
Nothing could save me.

Kensuke's Kingdom, Michael Morpurgo

Understanding the extract

1 What is the setting for the extract?

2 Why did Michael think Stella was barking?

3 Why did he pick up the dog?

4 Why did he think he was being 'silly'?

5 What two things frightened Michael when he was in the water?

Understanding the words

6 Explain the meaning of these words and phrases as they are used in
   the extract.

   a made redundant   b sweeten her   c lunged
   d still reluctant   e veered   f cruising

Exploring further

7 Explain in your own words why Michael 'shouldn't have left the wheel'.

8 Why do you think the ball was very 'precious' to him?

q How do you think Michael felt when he was plunged into 'the cold of the
   sea'?

10 How do you think Michael gets to safety?

Extra

Write a brief conversation between Michael's parents when they realise
he is missing.

WRITE

Before reading

- How would pupils feel about going around the world in a boat?

- What places would they like to visit?

- What would they miss about not living on land?

Reading

- Explain to the pupils that they are going to read an extract from *Kensuke's Kingdom*, a third Michael Morpurgo story.

- The extract can be read to the class by the teacher, by individuals in the class or individually.

Questions

Pupils answer the questions individually, drawing on what they have learnt from previous class work (*Teach*) and group work (*Talk*) about Michael Morpurgo's work.

Round-up

- Discuss the three extracts. In what ways are they similar? In what ways are they different?

- What do pupils think Michael Morpurgo knows a lot about and is interested in?

? Answer guidance

Understanding the extract

1 The setting is the Peggy Sue / the sea.

2 'Someone was singing out there in the darkness.'

3 The dog would not come when he called her and would not move when he tried to drag her by the collar.

4 He thought 'you haven't got your safety harness on, you haven't got your lifejacket on'.

5 'The lights of the Peggy Sue went away in the dark of the night' / 'I thought then of sharks cruising the black water beneath me'.

Understanding the words

6 a *made redundant*: no longer having a job because the work isn't there;

b *sweeten her*: make her obey;

c *lunged*: made a grab for;

d *reluctant*: not willing;

e *veered*: changed direction suddenly;

f *cruising*: moving slowly and easily.

Exploring further

7 Answers suggesting that the 'wheel' was what kept the boat on course. By leaving it, the boat would drift in any direction the sea pushed it.

8 Answers that suggest that it could be the only thing he had to play with / it reminded him of home, etc.

9 Individual answers using evidence from the text suggesting he was terrified ('the terrors came fast, one upon another').

10 Individual answers in which pupils can draw from evidence in the text or predict an imaginative means of survival.

Extra

Individual answers.

ICT

81

- When and where did the incident occur?
- What had happened?
- List the possible explanations given in the article.
- Explain the meaning of the words and phrases in **bold**.
- Why do you think the reporter writes about 'when' and 'where' the incident occurred before writing about the incident itself?
- The dogs would not go into the wood. Why do you think some people saw that as 'proof' of the 'devil theory'?
- Why do you think people wanted Sir Richard Owen's opinion?
- What impression do you get of Mrs Ruth Standish?
- Give examples from the report of a fact and an opinion.
- Do any of the explanations convince you? Why? Why not?

The Daily News

Late Edition

11th February 1855

Devilish Doings in Devon

By Henry Harris

This winter has been the coldest anyone can remember and, two nights ago, the night of the 9th February, was **no exception**. Many parts of the country experienced a heavy snowfall, including Devon where the River Exe froze over, trapping birds in the ice.

The people of Totnes and Littlehampton, however, had more to talk about than the weather when they awoke yesterday morning. Something very **bizarre** had happened – something that no one can quite explain.

The countryside was smooth and white from the overnight snowfall. As would be expected,

there were prints from birds and animals here and there. What was not expected was a trail of tracks, seemingly made by a creature with hooves walking on two legs, which stretched for miles across the countryside.

The strange tracks began in a garden in Totnes and covered about 100 miles before simply coming to an end in a field near Littlehampton. What could the explanation be? Many villagers in these parts are in no doubt. The cloven-hooved tracks are the **devil's work!**

Police were on the scene very quickly and began by investigating the tracks that led into a wood near Dawlish. Dogs were brought to **flush out** the wood but they refused

Police on the trail of a mysterious creature.

to go in, standing at the edge howling pitifully. Proof, say those who support the devil **theory**, that something very mysterious is **afoot**.

When asked for his opinion, the leading **naturalist** Sir Richard Owen suggested that a badger had made the tracks. As it normally moves by placing its hind legs in the marks left by its forelegs, this explains why the creature appeared

to be two-footed. Mr Sam Coombe, a local farmer, said, "That may explain the two feet, but it doesn't explain the hooves. I've never seen a badger with hooves."

Some explanations are truly weird! An **amateur naturalist** suggests that the tracks are those of a kangaroo. When this reporter asked him where the kangaroo could have come from he replied, "It probably escaped from a travelling zoo and then returned to its cage without anyone noticing."

Mrs Ruth Standish, a local schoolteacher, **dismisses** the whole thing as a **hoax**, saying that she wouldn't put it past some of the young people in the area to have thought up and **executed** the whole thing as a huge joke.

There are those in the area who are convinced that the tracks were made by a wild beast and have gone, armed with pitchforks, to hunt it down.

Others, however, feel there is a more **supernatural** explanation. They are bolting their doors and refusing to **venture** outside after

sunset. They are playing safe and, until a **rational** explanation is found, believe that on 9th February 1855, the devil walked in Devon.

Villagers find strange tracks in the snow.

Extracts

Devilish Doings in Devon Henry Harris

Islands of Fire

The Northern Lights Fantastic Penny Stretton

Planning

Journalistic writing

Objectives

Renewed Primary Literacy Framework Year 6

1 Speaking
• Use a range of oral techniques to present persuasive arguments.
• Use the technique of dialogic talk to explore ideas, topics or issues.

7 *Understanding and interpreting texts*
• Understand how writers use different structures to create coherence and impact.

Assessment focuses

AF2 Understand, describe, select or retrieve information, events or ideas from texts and use quotation and reference to text

L4 Identifies relevant points, supported by generally relevant text references.

L5 Clearly identifies relevant points from across a text and supports them by reference to the text.

AF4 Identify and comment on the structure and organisation of texts including grammatical and presentational features

L3–L5 Increasingly clearly identifies and comments on structure of the text.

Scottish Curriculum for Excellence: Literacy

Listening and Talking

Understanding, analysing, evaluating (third level)
Can distinguish fact from opinion and recognise influence.

Reading

Finding and using information (second / third / fourth levels)
Using knowledge of features of text types, can find, select and sort information and use this for different purposes.

TEACH

In this unit pupils are given the opportunity to investigate journalistic news reports and identify key features of this text type. The articles are linked in as much as they report on fantastic happenings of the natural and the supernatural!

 Before reading
• Discuss the concept of the 'supernatural' with pupils.
• What do they understand by this term?
• Do they think there is such a thing?

 Reading
• Explain to the pupils that they are going to read an article called 'Devilish Doings in Devon', which reports an incident for which there is no satisfactory explanation.
• The article can be read to the class by the teacher; aloud by individual children in turn, or in silence individually.

 After reading

Use the panel prompts in the Pupil Book as the basis of a class discussion.

• When and where did the incident occur?
The incident occurred on the 9th February 1855 in Devon.

• What had happened?
Footprints were found in the snow between Totnes and Littlehampton, made by a hooved creature, walking on two legs.

• List the possible explanations given in the article.
Explanations given include 'the devil's work', 'a badger', 'young people', etc.

• Explain the meaning of the words and phrases in bold.
no exception: *just the same;* **bizarre:** *weird / strange;* **flush out:** *to cause something to be revealed (from the wood);* **theory:** *possible explanation;* **afoot:** *happening;* **naturalist:** *someone who studies the natural world;* **amateur:** *a person who does something as a hobby; not paid;* **dismisses:** *shrugs off;* **hoax:** *trick;* **executed:** *pulled off;* **venture:** *go;* **rational:** *reasonable.*

• Why do you think the reporter writes about 'when' and 'where' the incident occurred before writing about the incident itself?
Answers that suggest this is background information that the reader wants to know.

• The dogs would not go into the wood. Why do you think some people saw that as 'proof' of the 'devil theory'?
Answers that suggest animals are said to be sensitive to anything strange.

• Why do you think people wanted Sir Richard Owen's opinion?
Answers suggesting that, as a leading naturalist, he might have an explanation.

• What impression do you get of Mrs Ruth Standish?
Answers that suggest she is not superstitious, she is level-headed and doesn't believe in 'nonsense'.

ICT

ISLANDS OF Fire

Tongatapu, in the Pacific Ocean to the west of Australia, lies in the island group known as Tonga. On Monday 16 March 2009, about seven miles from Tongatapu, an underwater volcano began erupting. By Wednesday 18 March, so much lava had been ejected that it had formed a new island. On Thursday 19 March, a huge earthquake measuring 7.9 on the Richter scale occurred.

Fear of imminent danger to the surrounding islands prompted the Tsunami Warning Centre to issue a serious alert. Luckily, no damage or loss of life was reported.

The new island is made from pumice that is formed when lava cools rapidly. It is very light and can float. Experts agree that the island will last several months or possibly a few years but, in time, it will be eroded by the sea. A spokesman for the team of scientists on their way to the new island said that they were going to observe the eruption and, when things had quietened down, measure the island.

As well as volcanic eruptions creating islands, they can also make islands virtually disappear. One of the most famous examples is Krakatoa off the southwest coast of Indonesia.

In 1883, Krakatoa covered an area of 23 square kilometres to a height of 450 metres above sea level. On 20 May, there were reports of a plume of smoke rising 10 kilometres above the island. Minor eruptions continued from May to August,

and on 27 August 1883, a series of huge volcanic eruptions occurred, resulting in most of the island being submerged 250 metres below sea level.

Reports at the time say that the final explosion was heard 4,500 kilometres away and caused 40-metre high tsunamis that completely submerged many small islands. The major islands of Java and Sumatra were devastated: whole towns and villages were destroyed and nearly all vegetation was stripped away. Shipping suffered a similar fate, most being destroyed in the enormous waves. The Berouw, a steamship in the area, was carried 10 metres above sea level and deposited a mile inland.

It has been estimated that over 36,000 people lost their lives, either from the volcanic eruption that rained down ash and produced lava flows that reached up to 700 °C, or from the ensuing tsunamis. As far away as the east coast of Africa, rafts of pumice were washed up, sometimes with a grizzly cargo of human remains.

And Krakatoa has not finished yet. On 29 December 1927 more eruptions took place and a new volcano emerged from the sea. Anak Krakatoa – Child of Krakatoa – which is rumbling to this day, seemingly readying itself for another earth-shattering eruption.

Island before 26 August 1883

0   3 km

▲Perboewatan   Anak Krakatau
Danan
▲Rakata
Krakatau Island

Krakatoa as it was before the and after the explosion.

An eruption of Anak Krakatoa.

Understanding the article

- The article reports three incidents. When and where does each take place?
- In what way are the first and second incidents:
  a similar   b different?
- Why are the team of scientists going to the new island?
- What caused the loss of life after the eruption of Krakatoa?

Looking at words

Explain the meaning of these words and phrases as they are used in the article.

a ejected   b Richter scale   c imminent   d eroded
e virtually   f submerged   g tsunamis   h ensuing

Exploring further

- In addition to the text, how has the writer helped the reader to understand the article?
- Give an example of a fact and an opinion.
- Why do you think the writer gives exact dates and measurements in the article?
- Why do you think that the number of people who died is only estimated?
- Make a list of questions you would like to ask about Krakatoa.

Extra

Plan an article about an imaginary island with a volcano that erupts. Make notes on:

- what facts you need
- whose opinion you would include
- how you would illustrate the article
- how you would lay out the article.

Krakatoa as it was before the explosion.

TEACH continued ...

- Give examples from the report of a fact and an opinion.

  An example of a fact: 'Many parts of the country experienced a heavy snowfall.' An example of an opinion: 'Mrs Ruth Standish ... dismisses the whole thing as a hoax'.

- Do any of the explanations convince you? Why? Why not?

  Individual answers.

Plenary

Use the plenary session to investigate the features of the report, for example, headline, organisation, fact and opinion, illustration.

TALK

Before reading

- Discuss volcanoes with the pupils.
- What famous volcanoes do they know about?

Reading

- Explain to the pupils that they are going to read an article called 'Islands of Fire' about the startling effects of volcanic eruptions.
- The article can be read to the class by the teacher, by individuals in the class or as a group.

Discussion group

In groups, pupils discuss the questions and make notes on their responses. Ensure pupils understand that they do not always have to agree.

Understanding the article

- The article reports three incidents. When and where does each take place?

  The incidents took place at: Tongatapu, 16–19 March 2009; Krakatoa, 20 May–27 August 1883; Krakatoa, 29 December 1927.

- In what way are the first and second incidents:

  a similar

  Each was caused by a volcanic eruption.

  b different?

  In the Tongatapu eruption, an island was created. In the Krakatoa eruption, most of the island was submerged (disappeared).

- Why are the team of scientists going to the new island?

  They are going to 'observe the eruption' and 'measure the island'.

- What caused the loss of life after the eruption of Krakatoa?

  The loss of life was caused by 'the volcanic eruption that rained down ash and produced lava flows that reached up to 700 °C' and from the 'ensuing tsunamis'.

Looking at words

Explain the meaning of these words and phrases as they are used in the article:

a ejected: *thrown up violently;* **b Richter scale:** *the scale that shows the strength of an earthquake;* **c imminent:** *immediate;* **d eroded:** *worn away;* **e virtually:** *almost;* **f submerged:** *under water;* **g tsunamis:** *sea waves caused by underwater earthquakes;* **h ensuing:** *following.*

Exploring further

- In addition to the text, how has the writer

---

helped the reader to understand the article?

Answers suggesting the use of photographs and maps.

- Give an example of a fact and an opinion.

  Individual answers – for example, fact: Tongatapu lies in the Pacific Ocean to the west of Australia; opinion: the island will last several months or a few years.

- Why do you think the writer gives exact dates and measurements in the article?

  Answers suggesting that readers will want to know exact facts of what is being written about, not just vague guesses. A hallmark of good journalistic writing is research.

- Why do you think that the number of people who died is only estimated?

  Answers suggesting that it would have been impossible to actually count the number of dead as there were so many, with many bodies never found.

- Make a list of questions you would like to ask about Krakatoa.

  Ensure all members of the group contribute questions.

Extra

Ensure all members of the group contribute to the content and layout of the article.

Plenary

- Use the pupils' list of questions about Krakatoa as the basis for a class discussion.
- Let groups read each other's articles and comment critically on them. Point out where journalistic features have been used to good effect.

The Northern Lights Fantastic

by Penny Stretton

The Northern Lights sweep startling colours across the frozen night sky as the moon rises over the snow.

A shock of yellow lights up the mountains in Yukon, Canada, threatening to outshine the full moon.

In the nearby Brooks Range, a glow of turquoise and pink bathe an igloo in unearthly light.

And waves of green dance around a streak of white and pink high above an Eskimo monument, or inukshuk, in Hudson Bay, Manitoba.

Photographer Rolf Hicker has spent the last 10 years travelling thousands of miles with his wife Michelle to capture these amazing images.

The Aurora Borealis is only visible at night, and is best seen in winter. It is extremely difficult to capture the full glory of the Northern Lights, especially with a full moon – and most photographers

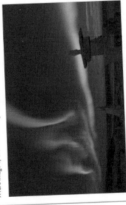

An Eskimo inukshuk is illuminated by waves of green dancing lights

A rare image of the Northern Lights with a full moon.

don't bother. But Mr Hicker found a way. He said, 'It's the perfect time to show the Northern Lights with the landscape. If conditions are right, especially when it is very cold, you can experience one of the most amazing moments we ever have – a moonrise with the Aurora Borealis, all at the same time.'

He added: 'The reward for all the trouble is amazing – silence and dancing Northern Lights in the moonlight.'

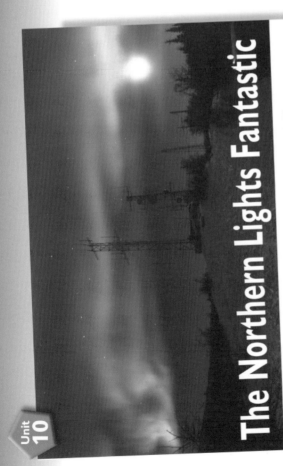

An igloo looks startlingly white lit up by a flash of turquoise and pink.

Understanding the article

1 Name the three places the photographer has visited to photograph the Northern Lights.
2 What is the other name for the Northern Lights?
3 How many years have Mr Hicker and his wife been travelling to 'capture these amazing images'?
4 What are the best conditions to see the Northern Lights?

Understanding the words

5 Explain the meaning of these words as they are used in the article.

a startling   b threatening   c outshine
d bathe   e unearthly   f visible

Exploring further

6 Why do you think the Northern Lights are 'best seen in winter'?
7 What impression do you get of Rolf Hicker?
8 Why do you think most photographers 'don't bother' to try to photograph the Northern Lights?
9 Would the article be as interesting without the photographs? Why? Why not?
10 Explain how you think Rolf Hicker feels when he is watching the Northern Lights. How would you feel?

Extra

Imagine you could interview Rolf Hicker about his travels and photography. What questions would you like to ask him?

 **Before reading**

- What do pupils understand by the term 'Northern Lights'?
- Have any pupils seen them?

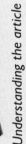 **Reading**

- Explain to the pupils that they are going to read an article called 'The Northern Lights Fantastic', where a reporter interviews a photographer who has spent many years photographing the Northern Lights.

- The article can be read to the class by the teacher, by individuals in the class or individually.

 Questions

Pupils answer the questions individually, drawing on what they have learnt from previous class work (*Teach*) and group work (*Talk*) about the features of journalistic writing.

Round-up

- Use pupils' answers to the 'Extra' activity as the basis for a class discussion.

- Review with the pupils what they understand by 'journalistic writing'.

 Answer guidance

Understanding the article

1 Mountains of Yukon; Brooks Range; Hudson Bay.
2 Aurora Borealis.
3 Ten years.
4 The Northern Lights are best seen 'at night … in winter'.

Understanding the words

5 a *startling*: surprising;
 b *threatening*: suggesting they could;
 c *outshine*: be brighter than;
 d *bathe*: cover;
 e *unearthly*: mysterious;
 f *visible*: able to be seen.

Exploring further

6 Answers suggesting that it is darker earlier in winter and that a cloudless sky (as on a frosty night) will make them easier to see.

7 Answers that suggest Rolf Hicker is dedicated / almost obsessive / a very good photographer.
8 Answers suggesting that it is very difficult to get good photographs of them.
9 Individual answers suggesting that it would not be as interesting because the photographs show the beauty and strangeness of the Northern Lights that the reader would not appreciate without them.
10 Individual answers suggesting that he feels wonder / awe / amazement. Children may feel the same.

Extra

Individual answers.

Name _____ Class _____ Date _____

		Type	AF	Mark
1	When did Mandy have the first dream?	Literal	AF2	/1
2	Who did she go to talk to after the first dream?	Literal	AF2	/1
3	What did the girl in the dream look like?	Literal	AF2	/1
4	At what point did Mandy wake up: **a** in the first dream _____ **b** in the second dream? _____	Inference	AF3	/2
5	Explain the meaning of these words and phrases as they are used in the extract: **a** awoke _____ **b** nightmare _____ **c** unruly _____ **d** reluctantly _____ **e** silent movies _____ **f** ridiculous _____	Clarification	AF3	/6
6	Find evidence in the extract to show how Mandy reacted to the first dream.	Inference	AF3	/2
7	Why do you think Mandy told her brother about her dream but not her parents?	Evaluation – empathy	AF6	/3
8	What impression do you get of Mandy?	Evaluation – opinion	AF6	/3
9	How do you think Mandy's parents will react now that they know about the dreams?	Evaluation – prediction	AF6	/3
10	Do you think Mandy was more or less frightened the second time she had the dream? Explain your reasons.	Evaluation – empathy	AF6	/3

Unit 1 – Things that go bump in the night!
Unit objective: Exploring atmosphere and tension

Total marks: /25

© Nelson Thornes 2009

Name _____ Class _____ Date _____

		Type	AF	Mark
1	Where and when was Louis Braille born?	Literal	AF2	/1
2	What did his father do?	Literal	AF2	/1
3	What happened to Louis when: **a** he was three years old _____ **b** he was ten years old _____ **c** he was twenty years old? _____	Literal – summarising	AF2	/3
4	Explain the meaning of the highlighted words and phrases as they are used in the extract: **a** harnesses _____ **b** infected _____ **c** bulky _____ **d** consisted of _____ **e** less complicated _____	Clarification	AF3	/5
5	In what ways do you think only being able to listen to your teacher and not being able to read and write notes would be difficult?	Evaluation – previous experience	AF6	/3
6	Explain in your own words how 'night writing' worked.	Summarising	AF2	/4
7	What impression do you get of Louis Braille from this biography?	Evaluation – opinion	AF6	/3
8	There are eight paragraphs in the biography. Write briefly what each one is about.	Summarising	AF3	/8
9	How is the biography organised?	Analysis – text structure	AF4	/3

Name _____ Class _____ Date _____

		Type	AF	Mark
1	Find three things normally found on land that the coral reef says it is.	Literal	AF2	/3
2	What do 'frightened fishes' use the coral reef for?	Literal	AF2	/1
3	What choice do people have to make about coral reefs?	Literal	AF2	/1
4	Explain the meaning of these words as they are used in the poem: **a** teeming _____ **b** skeleton _____ **c** predators _____ **d** luminous _____ **e** brittle _____ **f** heirloom _____	Clarification	AF3	/6
5	Explain what the poet means when she says that the coral reef is: **a** 'built on / Uncountable small deaths' _____ _____ **b** 'An endlessly growing sculpture' _____	Analysis – language use	AF5	/6
6	What do you think the 'unseen monsters' are?	Inference	AF3	/2
7	Why do you think the towers are described as 'improbable'?	Evaluation – opinion	AF6	/3
8	The poet has given the coral reef a voice. What warning is the coral reef giving to the reader?	Evaluation – author view point	AF6	/3
9	If the coral reef was human, what sort of person do you think it would be?	Evaluation – opinion	AF6	/3

Unit 3 – Painting a picture
Unit objective: Understanding themes and recognising personification

Total marks: /28

Name _____ Class _____ Date _____

		Type	AF	Mark
1	What has John Hammond done?	Literal	AF2	/1
2	Where are the characters at the beginning of the extract?	Literal	AF2	/1
3	Why could the T-rex grip the fence?	Literal	AF2	/1
4	What does Gennaro do when he sees the T-rex?	Literal	AF1	/1
5	Why does Alan say, 'Don't move'?	Literal	AF1	/1
6	Explain the meaning of these words as they are used in the context of the extract: **a** quaking _____ **b** vibrations _____ **c** bolted _____ **d** beacon _____ **e** butted _____ **f** undercarriage _____	Clarification	AF3	/6
7	How does the author create a feeling of fear in the first three paragraphs?	Analysis – language use	AF5	/3
8	What impression do you get of Gennaro?	Evaluation – opinion	AF6	/3
9	How do you know that Dr Alan Grant knows something about dinosaurs?	Inference	AF3	/2
10	Why do you think Lex turned on the flashlight?	Evaluation – empathy	AF6	/3

Name _____ Class _____ Date _____

		Type	AF	Mark
1	Where and when do UFO 'sightings' usually take place?	Literal	AF2	/1
2	When were UFOs first sighted?	Literal	AF2	/1
3	In the fourth paragraph, what is the writer puzzled about?	Literal	AF2	/1
4	In your own words, explain what happened recently at Cirencester College.	Summarising	AF2	/2
5	Explain the meaning of these words and phrases as they are used in the article: **a** abducted _____ **b** rural _____ **c** physical evidence _____ **d** Venusians _____ **e** space probe _____ **f** superior technology _____	Clarification	AF3	/6
6	What is the purpose of: **a** the first paragraph _____ _____ **b** the article as a whole? _____	Analysis – text structure	AF4	/4
7	Who do you think is the intended audience?	Evaluation – author viewpoint	AF6	/3
8	The writer repeats the fact that most UFO 'sightings' are reported by people who are alone. What is the writer implying?	Inference	AF3	/2
9	Does the writer want the final paragraph to be taken seriously or not? Explain your reasons.	Evaluation – author viewpoint	AF6	/3
10	Are you convinced by the writer's arguments? Why? Why not?	Evaluation – criticism	AF6	/3

Unit 5 – Which side are you on?
Unit objective: Understanding the conventions of argument

Total marks: /26

© Nelson Thornes 2009

Finding a voice

Name _____ Class _____ Date _____

		Type	AF	Mark
1	What is the setting for the poem?	Literal	AF2	/1
2	What smells does the poet notice?	Literal	AF2	/1
3	When the poet was 'pinned to the wall', what was he about to do?	Literal	AF2	/1
4	When did the poet's 'fear' die?	Literal	AF2	/1
5	Explain the meaning of these words and phrases as they are used in the poem: **a** atmosphere _____ **b** shattering _____ **c** pursued _____ **d** on the verge _____ **e** timidly _____	Clarification	AF3	/5
6	Find evidence in the poem that tells you how the boy was feeling at the beginning of the poem.	Inference	AF3	/2
7	Find evidence that tells you how he was feeling at the end of the poem.	Inference	AF3	/2
8	What impression is the poet trying to create with the words 'barged, 'banged' and 'pushing and shoving'?	Analysis – language use	AF5	/3
9	Do you think the boys were being deliberately unkind to the poet? Why? Why not?	Evaluation – empathy	AF6	/3
10	There are 'Boys and still more boys' in the school. Why do you think it took only one boy being kind to the poet to make him feel better?	Evaluation – empathy	AF6	/3

Name _____ Class _____ Date _____

		Type	AF	Mark
1	Name the two men climbing in the Andes.	Literal	AF2	/1
2	Which mountain were they climbing?	Literal	AF2	/1
3	Which side of the mountain were they on?	Literal	AF2	/1
4	What could a minor injury, such as a broken ankle, mean for only two climbers on a mountain?	Literal	AF2	/1
5	Explain the meaning of these words and phrases as they are used in the extract: **a** locked **b** catapulted **c** grotesque distortion **d** nausea **e** ruptured **f** impact	Clarification	AF3	/6
6	What do you think Joe means when he says, 'Simon would be ripped off the mountain. He couldn't hold this'?	Evaluation – author viewpoint	AF6	/3
7	Joe says, 'My thoughts raced madly'. What 'thoughts' do you think were going through his mind at this point?	Evaluation – empathy	AF6	/3
8	Explain, in your own words, what the 'something dark with dread' was that occurred to Joe.	Evaluation – empathy	AF6	/3
9	Joe's right leg was injured. Why do you think he kicked it 'against the slope'?	Evaluation – empathy	AF6	/3
10	What impression do you get of Joe Simpson?	Evaluation – opinion	AF6	/3

Unit 7 – Daring deeds
Unit objective: Explore how writers present experiences

Total marks: /25

© Nelson Thornes 2009

Name _____ Class _____ Date _____

		Type	AF	Mark
1	How old is the Tower of London?	Literal – finding information	AF2	/1
2	Who saw the ghosts of the two princes?	Literal – finding information	AF2	/1
3	Which ghost appears more than any other?	Literal – finding information	AF2	/1
4	Which is the most haunted area of the Tower?	Literal – finding information	AF2	/1
5	Explain the meaning of these words and phrases as they are used in the guide: **a** the story goes _____ **b** appease _____ **c** future king _____ **d** persist _____ **e** pursued _____ **f** re-enacting _____ **g** bayonet _____ **h** apparition _____	Clarification	AF3	/8
6	What evidence is there in the guide to show that Henry III probably believed in ghosts?	Inference – deducing information	AF3	/2
7	What do you understand about the story of the princes in the Tower from the phrase 'Tradition says'?	Analysis – language use	AF5	/3
8	Why do you think the ghost of Anne Boleyn appears 'headless'?	Evaluation – historical knowledge	AF7	/3
9	What do most of these ghosts have in common?	Inference	AF3	/2
10	Why do you think the writer has included these ghost stories in the guide?	Evaluation – author viewpoint	AF6	/3

Danger at sea!

Assessme

Name _____ Class _____ Date _____

		Type	AF	Mark
1	What is the setting for the extract?	Literal	AF2	/1
2	Why did Michael think Stella was barking?	Literal	AF2	/1
3	Why did he pick up the dog?	Inference	AF3	/2
4	Why did he think he was being 'silly'?	Literal	AF2	/1
5	What two things frightened Michael when he was in the water?	Inference	AF2	/2
6	Explain the meaning of these words and phrases as they are used in the extract: **a** made redundant _____ **b** sweeten her _____ **c** lunged _____ **d** still reluctant _____ **e** veered _____ **f** cruising _____	Clarification	AF3	/6
7	Explain, in your own words, why Michael 'shouldn't have left the wheel'.	Evaluation – previous experience	AF6	/3
8	Why do you think the ball was very 'precious' to him?	Evaluation – empathy	AF6	/3
9	How do you think Michael felt when he was plunged into 'the cold of the sea'?	Evaluation – empathy	AF6	/3
10	How do you think Michael gets to safety?	Evaluation – prediction	AF6	/3

Unit 9 – Danger at sea!
Unit objective: Understanding an author's themes and techniques

Total marks: /25

Name _____ Class _____ Date _____

		Type	AF	Mark
1	Name the three places the photographer has visited to photograph the Northern Lights.	Literal	AF2	/1
2	What is the other name for the Northern Lights?	Inference	AF3	/2
3	How many years have Mr Hicker and his wife been travelling to 'capture these amazing images'?	Literal	AF3	/1
4	What are the best conditions to see the Northern Lights?	Literal	AF2	/1
5	Explain the meaning of these words as they are used in the article: **a** startling _____ **b** threatening _____ **c** outshine _____ **d** bathe _____ **e** unearthly _____ **f** visible _____	Clarification	AF3	/6
6	Why do you think the Northern Lights are 'best seen in winter'?	Inference	AF3	/2
7	What impression do you get of Rick Hicker?	Evaluation – opinion	AF6	/3
8	Why do you think most photographers 'don't bother' to try to photograph the Northern Lights?	Evaluation – opinion	AF3	/3
9	Would the article be as interesting without the photographs? Why? Why not?	Analysis – text structure	AF4	/3
10	Explain how you think Rick Hicker feels when he is watching the Northern Lights. How would you feel?	Evaluation – empathy	AF6	/3

Using the Picture Snapshot Assessment

Donna Thomson

Reading and interpreting images provides a powerful and stimulating comprehension teaching and assessment tool for children of all ages and abilities. Pictures are full of inferred and hidden meaning and are a good starting point for comprehension instruction. This is because literal, inferential and evaluative visual clues are more immediate and easier to identify than text clues. Pictures can activate prior knowledge and experience in an instant. They prompt a range of emotions and personal reactions that absorb children and invite them to investigate and enquire further. The explicit teaching involved in the 'Snapshot Assessment' process helps children to develop essential thinking skills that can be transferred to other learning areas across the curriculum.

Picture Snapshot Assessment format

The 'Picture Snapshot Assessment' is an integral part of the Nelson Comprehension CD-ROMs. It provides an intriguing range of fiction and non-fiction stills and animated images with sound effects, accompanied by questions and answer guidance to test and assess a child's comprehension skills. The format is easy for pupils to use individually or in collaborative ability – or mixed-ability teams of two to five pupils. It is also designed for teachers to use as a smart board instruction model. We have related the pictures to the APP assessment focuses 2 to 7 and have grouped them in levels which approximate to National Curriculum reading levels 1 to 5.

Assessing strengths and weaknesses

Pupils' responses to the questions, and their own enquiry about 'Snapshot' picture narratives, offer teachers an excellent opportunity to assess their comprehension strengths and weaknesses. Assessment focus indicators that accompany each 'Snapshot' level provide teachers with a guide for assessment evidence gathered during each session. 'Snapshot' also assesses the comprehension skills of struggling decoders and pupils with language difficulties. The assessment process is effective because the absence of text (other than the title of a picture) allows the pupil the freedom to focus on comprehending, interpreting and choosing their own words to describe what is happening in a story, rather than on their struggle with decoding, which impedes their ability to understand the story in any depth.

Comprehension strategies

The 'Snapshot' activities are based on the Reciprocal Reading framework (Palicsar and Brown, 1986), a teacher-modelled scaffold that supports children's independent enquiry of fiction and non-fiction. Similarly, the 'Snapshots' are designed as an interactive process that helps children to read meaning within pictures, using the key comprehension strategies of summarising, predicting, questioning and clarifying. These key strategies draw on all assessment focuses except AF1. They encourage groups of the same or mixed ability pupils to delve deeply into picture narrative: extending their vocabulary, clarifying meaning and justifying viewpoints. It also helps them to develop the language of response and debate as they answer and generate their own literal, inferential and evaluative questions to monitor their understanding.

Using snapshots with small groups

While 'Snapshot' assessment is ideal for one-to-one assessment, it can also be used highly effectively with small groups of pupils. If the teams are unable to collaborate effectively, the groups will achieve little from the interactive activities. It can be very useful to define a specific role for each of the five to six pupils in the group (for example, a reader for the title and questions, a scribe, somebody to report back to the class, and someone to challenge their initial answers). The team members can take it in turns to experience these roles as they move through the different levels.

How 'Snapshot' works

Each picture still and animated sequence is specifically selected to assess pupils' ability to use key comprehension strategies to answer questions and generate their own questions. The titles of the images relate to the picture and sound clues that are linked to the picture narrative. The purpose of this is to encourage the reader to link the word clues to the images and sounds to explain what is happening and to predict narrative outcomes.

Hotspots
The clues in the picture narrative that tell the reader 'what is happening', 'what may have happened before' or 'what may happen next' are referred to in the series as 'hotspots'. Teachers and children are able to confirm the meaning of each clue by clicking directly on the hotspot to reveal the information. These clues range from literal 'who?', 'what?, 'where?' information, to inferred

suggestions that require the reader to search for other clues to show how they have arrived at a conclusion, or why they think the characters are thinking or feeling in a certain way in the scene.

Screen 1 – section of whole image

The procedure on each level is progressive and extremely supportive. It begins with only part of the whole image shown on screen to encourage the reader to search for clues and link them to the title to predict what might be happening in the 'bigger picture' (rather like predicting contents from the cover of a book). The delving process also involves three literal questions that provide the basic information about the character(s), what they are doing and where they are; an evaluation question that asks them to consider what the characters might be feeling or thinking from their expression and body language; and a prediction question that asks them to calculate from the clues revealed what the story or 'whole scene' might be about.

Screen 1
Snapshot non-fiction level 5

Screen 2 – whole image

The next scene reveals the whole picture and asks the reader to look carefully at new clues. The initial questions are revisited to allow the reader to revise their previous view of what is happening as they answer again. Finally, there are two prediction questions that help them to consider what might have happened before and after the 'whole picture' scene.

Screen 2
Snapshot non-fiction level 5

Assessment grid

The assessment at the end focuses on the accumulated answers to questions from screens 1 and 2, together with additional questions that ask the reader to generate their own query from a given answer to further assess their understanding and to measure their ability to ask literal, inference and evaluation questions. The final assessment score indicates possible areas for teacher intervention.

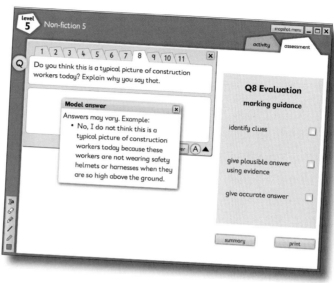

It is during the process of gathering and linking information to answer questions – and attempts at generating their own questions – that pupils' comprehension strengths and weaknesses are first exposed and the pupils themselves are able to identify areas of difficulty or lack of confidence. Throughout the process they are supported as they learn how to make links and connections between high and low levels of information.

Each assessment question is supported by a model answer and marking guidance.

'Snapshot' activities

The following levelled fiction and non-fiction 'snapshot' picture activities are designed to present a range of high- and low-level visual and sound clues that become more complex as the levels progress. Some are illustrations, others are black and white or colour photographs and many of them are animated. The purpose of these activities is to show children how to gather, clarify and organise information, how to identify the difference between literal and inferred meaning and how to make links and connections to solve problems. The animated clues have been included to draw the reader's eye to the hotspot information. The range of generic questions presented on each screen model a line of enquiry that the children soon learn and transfer to other areas of learning.

The first screen presents part of a whole picture. The reader first needs to read the title then look carefully at the picture for hotspot clues and listen for sound effects that suggest what may be happening in the narrative. The children's enquiry is guided by a series of questions that help them to gather information and make links of meaning between the clues on screens 1 and 2. The second screen shows the whole picture and includes further questions to support enquiry. These clues also provide confirmation of earlier predictions.

Snapshot: Level 1 Fiction – 'Halloween' (RA 5 yrs–6.5 yrs)

Visual type	Description
Colour illustration with some animation and sound effects	A pleasant looking woman is sitting in her cottage at the table pouring tea. It is night-time. Behind the woman we see children passing by, dressed in scary costumes. There are strange things happening in the room. There is loud banging at the door.

Screen information

Screen 1 – shows part of the whole picture

Hotspot clues: Black cat stirring pot, pouring green tea, children in ghost and skeleton outfits, lit pumpkin, moon in sky.

Sound clues: Bubbling cauldron, tea pouring, children's muffled laughter and chatter, loud banging on the door.

Screen 2 – the whole picture

Hotspot clues: Children in skeleton and monster costumes, witch's hat and cloak, Halloween date on calendar – 31st October, walking butter dish, sweeping broom, jar of sweets and jar of spiders.

Sound clues: Loud banging on door, children's voices shouting 'trick or treat', 'swish' sound of brush on floor occasionally.

What is happening?

The clues indicate that the children are 'trick-or-treating' because the title says it is Halloween. The children are dressed up in scary clothes and they are banging on the door and shouting 'trick-or-treat'. The clues also imply that the woman is a witch because of the hat and cloak on the door and strange goings-on in the house. The children are asked to consider what might happen if the witch opens the door to the children.

Snapshot: Level 1 Non-Fiction – 'Making Pizza' (RA 5 yrs–6.5 yrs)

Visual type	Description
Colour photograph with some sound effects	Four people working in a pizza factory.

Screen information

Screen 1 – shows part of the whole picture

Hotspot clues: Girl in white coat, plastic hat, mouth covered, man holding olives in gloved hand, machinery, pizza.

Sound clues (screens 1 and 2): Background radio music, sound of machinery and movement of production line, occasional cough, muffled voice counting 1 … 2 … 3 … 4!

Screen 2 – the whole picture

Hotspot clues: Pizza with four olives on, woman's hand reaching to put olives on bare pizza.

What is happening?

The clues indicate that the people are workers in a pizza factory because they are wearing protective clothing for hygiene reasons. They are all putting the same number of olives on pizzas in a line. There is the sound of machinery in the background and the title says 'Making Pizza'.

Snapshot: Level 2 Fiction – 'A Roundabout Ride' (RA 6.5 yrs–8.5 yrs)

Visual type	Description
Colour illustration with some animations	Outside a zoo by a funfair two zoo keepers are searching for something in the bushes. Children are running towards the roundabout ride. There is a tiger standing on the roundabout.

Screen information

Screen 1 – shows part of the whole picture

Hotspot clues: Sign pointing to zoo, zoo keeper with net, zoo keeper moving branch to peer into shrub, large paw prints, helter skelter ride.

Sound clues (screens 1 and 2): Fairground music, children laughing and squealing, tiger licking lips, smacking sound, girl's excited voice saying 'I want to go on the tiger ride!'

Screen 2 – the whole picture

Hotspot clues: Girl pointing at roundabout, end of tiger's tail twitching, tiger licking lips, girl on zebra ride looking worried, worried onlookers, excited children running up to roundabout.

What is happening?

The clues indicate that the two zoo keepers are looking for a tiger that has escaped from the zoo, because there are large paw prints leading to the roundabout where a tiger is standing. The tiger is pretending to be a ride on the roundabout either to avoid being caught by the zoo keepers, or because he is hungry and wants to trick a child into riding him so he can eat them – he is licking his lips. The reader is asked to consider what might happen next. Will the frightened onlookers tell the zoo keepers about the tiger before the children reach him?

Snapshot: Level 2 Non-Fiction – 'Dog Grooming' (RA 6.5 yrs–8.5 yrs)

Visual type	Description
Colour Illustration with some sound effects	The scene shows dogs being spruced up in a dog grooming parlour.

Screen information

Screen 1 – shows part of the whole picture

Hotspot clues: Perfect-looking poodle, dirty and scruffy-looking dog, 'Posh Paws' writing backwards on glass door, dog owner coming in – expression on his face (comparing the two dogs), dog owner going out – expression on her face (comparing the two dogs).

Sound clues (screens 1 and 2): Buzz of electric trimmer, sound of shower spray, voice saying 'Good dog', dog barking, dog whining.

Screen 2 – the whole picture

Hotspot clues: Two dogs ready to go home, electric trimmer, clipped fur (falling chunks of hair), girl's uniform ('Posh Paws' logo), man holding shower head, all dogs (except one in bath) have wagging tails.

What is happening?

The clues indicate that this is a place where dogs are washed and have their fur trimmed. The wagging tails tell us that most of them enjoy the experience, except the dog being showered. The clues further suggest that the dog owners take pride in the appearance of their dogs. The owner coming in looks embarrassed that his dog is so dirty compared to the perfect poodle going out.

Snapshot: Level 3 Fiction – 'All at Sea' (RA 8.5 yrs–10.5 yrs)

Visual type	Description
Animated colour illustration with sound effects	A boat has overturned in a choppy sea. A man who was hanging on in the water is now sitting on top of the boat calling for help. There is a man in a small boat nearby who is pulling another man out of the water. A person is watching from the shore.

Screen information

Screen 1 – shows part of the whole picture

Hotspot clues: overturned boat, hand clutching boat rope, top of head (turning to look at other boat), wave swell, floating apple, lunchbox, floating oar, life jacket, lightning/dark clouds, seagulls.

Sound clues: Seagulls crying, voice in panic to himself 'Oh no, it's getting closer', sound of wind/waves/sea.

Screen 2 – the whole picture

Hotspot clues: Frightened man jumps up onto boat, shark's fin circling boat, man pulling swimmer into boat, man swimming towards boat, person watching on shore.

Sound clues: Voice shouts out 'Help – over here!', sound of wind/waves/sea, seagulls crying, oar banging against boat.

What is happening?

The clues indicate that two men are out for the day and were just about to have lunch when their boat was overturned during a bad storm. Further clues suggest that a man in a small boat has come from the shore to rescue them, because someone is watching from the shore as he pulls one of the men into the boat. Another clue implies that the man who is calling for help may not be a strong swimmer, because unlike the other man, he has chosen not to swim to safety. The reader is asked to consider what might happen to him in the end.

Snapshot: Level 3 Non-Fiction – 'Fish for Dinner' (RA 8.5 yrs–10.5 yrs)

Visual type	Description
Black and white photograph with sound effects	Two men are in a moored boat and a dog is watching them from a jetty.

Screen information

Screen 1 – shows part of the whole picture

Hotspot clues: Boat tied to mooring post, heaped rocks, fishing rod, hatch cover, dog with collar looking at something going on.

Sound clues (screens 1 and 2): 'Swish' sound of line being cast, 'plop!' sound as hook and bait hit the water, men talking in French, sighing and chuckling, whining sound.

Screen 2 – the whole picture

Hotspot clues: Man sitting on left of boat, man sitting on chair smoking pipe, old-fashioned bamboo fishing rod, old-fashioned containers, man wearing French beret.

What is happening?

The sound clues indicate that the two men in the moored boat are French and out fishing for the day. The photograph is black and white, which suggests it is a scene from the past, and the men are smoking pipes and using old-fashioned equipment to fish with. The title implies that the men are not the only ones expecting fish for dinner – the dog is whining and looks like he is waiting for something as he watches them fishing.

Snapshot: Level 4 Fiction – 'Good Fit' (RA 10.5 yrs–11.5 yrs)

Visual type	Description
Colour illustrations with sound effects	There are four little men in the scene looking at a diagram, another is posing with a duck, two more are carrying a large roll of material, some are sewing and others are measuring. There is a giant pair of feet standing in the background.

Screen information

Screen 1 – shows part of the whole picture

Hotspot clues: Diagram of large man, spotted material, foreign language, pet duck on a lead, man puzzling over diagram and carefully observing something, large roll of spotted material.

Sound clues (screens 1 and 2): Snipping scissors, foreign muttering as background, other occasional voices ('mmmmh', sigh) thinking aloud, occasional quack.

Screen 2 – the whole picture

Hotspot clues: Pet duck on lead, big roll of spotted material, small man with megaphone, enormous shoe, hole in stocking, small men with needles working on material.

What is happening?
The clues indicate that some little people are making new clothes for a giant because they are working from a clothes pattern designed for a large man. They are measuring, cutting and sewing big pieces of material to fit him. Also the story is entitled 'Good Fit'.

Screen 3 – the story conclusion

Image of giant being measured for clothes by little people.

Snapshot: Level 4 Non-Fiction – 'World Championships 2008' (RA 10.5 yrs–11.5 yrs)

Visual type	Description
Colour photograph	Children and adults in a crowd watching a snail racing event.

Screen information

Screen 1 – shows part of the whole picture

Hotspot clues: Man shouting, expressions on faces of crowd – their age and gender, fence of flags.

Sound clues (screens 1 and 2): Male shouting 'Ready, steady, slow!' followed by background sound of small crowd talking, cheering and laughing occasionally.
In foreground, male and female voices shouting 'Come on, come on!'
Child's voice (laughing) 'That's the wrong way!'

Screen 2 – the whole picture

Hotspot clues: Outer red circle, inner red circle, snail moving inside circle, snail moving towards outer red line.

What is happening?
Clues indicate that people are racing snails in an important race because the photograph is entitled 'World Championships 2008' and there is a small crowd of spectators cheering on some snails that are moving across a table. Other clues imply that it is a race because all the snails are placed on a starting line in the centre of the tablecloth, and most of them are heading for the red line at the edge of the cloth, which suggests the finishing line of a race.

Snapshot: Level 5 Fiction – 'The Tea Picker' (RA 11.5 yrs–12.5 yrs)

Visual type	Description
Colour illustration	On a plantation set in an exotic landscape, the scene shows three women in Indian dress with large baskets on their backs. They are watching a well-dressed man sneering as he stands over a small girl who is weeping beside an overturned basket.

Screen information

Screen 1 – shows part of the whole picture

Screen 2 – the whole picture

What is happening?

Clues indicate that the scene is taking place on a tea plantation because the title refers to 'tea pickers', the women are carrying baskets and the little girl's overturned basket contains some leaves. Sound clues suggest that the girl is weeping because the overseer is sneering at her, either for dropping the large basket or because she has picked such a small amount. The reader is asked to consider what might happen next to the young girl.

Hotspot clues: Foreign landscape, concerned looking woman in Indian dress, authoritative man looking at ground, crops, shadow.

Sound clues (screens 1 and 2): Tropical sounds, Indian voices (women murmuring concern), man making 'humph!' sneering sound, child sniffing (weeping).

Hotspot clues: Women with baskets looking away and talking quietly together, tea leaves on the ground, tipped over basket, girl hanging head down, girl's foot curled awkwardly, man's hands on hips, man's facial expression.

Snapshot: Level 5 Non-Fiction – 'Making Manhattan' (RA 11.5 yrs–12.5 yrs)

Visual type	Description
Black and white photograph with sound effects	A line of workmen are sitting having a lunch break high above a city landscape.

Screen information

Screen 1 – shows part of the whole picture

Screen 2 – the whole picture

What is happening?

The men are probably skyscraper construction workers because they are sitting on a steel girder high above a city of very tall buildings. Also the photograph is entitled 'Making Manhattan' which implies they are working on a Manhattan city building. The workers are all probably American because Manhattan is in the USA and there are also skyscrapers in America. Clues further imply that the photograph is a scene from the past because of the lack of safety equipment, the old-fashioned clothes the men are wearing, and the quality of the black and white photograph. Readers may wonder why the men are so relaxed sitting high above the ground when they are not protected from falling.

Hotspot clues: Cap, dungarees, lunch box, buildings in background, steel cable, vest.

Sound clues (screens 1 and 2): Sound of wind, male chatter and laughter.

Hotspot clues: Two men lighting a cigarette (far left), work gloves (second on left), feet dangling, skyscrapers below.

Analysing responses to questions

Gathering information, discussing and retelling is an essential part of the comprehension process. It is the first indicator of a reader's real engagement and basic understanding of the text or picture narrative. It shows how observant they are and what sort of reasoning skills they have. If they haven't grasped the main ideas when summarising the story information, the indications are that they are not looking closely enough; have poor language skills (vocabulary/phrasing) and sequencing ability; or have little personal or prior experience that links to the information in the picture. They may, as a consequence, give limited answers to the following questions about the picture narrative. The teacher may choose to give the individual or team a less demanding (lower level) picture to work from.

In the process of determining whether a student has answered a question correctly, the teacher needs to consider the following points.

- Does the reader's answer relate to the information in the title and picture?
- Is prior knowledge or experience being used to help explain a picture narrative?
- Does the reader understand the vocabulary used in the question?
- Does the reader have problems gathering literal or inferred information in response to questions?
- Does the reader have problems making links between clues to arrive at a conclusion?
- Is the reader engaged in the picture narrative?

Analysing responses to question types

Example: Level 4 'Good Fit' (Screen 2 picture)

Literal – explicit meaning – Who?, What?, Where? Right there! Information that is obvious and does not require interpretation.

Literal questions ask for answers that are found directly on the page. This simple form of questioning is essential when assessing whether a reader understands how to link key enquiry words in a question to basic key information within the text.

An example of a poor response to a literal question:

Question: *What* are the characters *doing* with the large roll of *material*?

Answer: The characters are making clothes.

Comment

The answer given here is an inferred response rather than an answer to a literal question. An inference question would need to include 'How do you know that?' to elicit this answer and evidence from the reader to support it.

The detail is clear in the picture. Although the reader has understood that many of the characters are *doing* something with material, they have not read the question carefully enough to identify who the question is directed at. The enquiry refers to the 'characters with the large roll of material' in the foreground of the picture and asks *what <u>they</u> are doing*.

> Correct answer: The *characters* are **carrying** the *large roll of material*.

Inference/Prediction – implied/hidden meaning. Information that is suggested within the narrative. The reader is required to think and search for clues that offer evidence to back up their response to questions.

Inference is not a straightforward question type. Although it allows for a variety of answers, all responses require evidence that relates to the picture or text information (in the title) and illustrator's/photographer's intention to support their answers. Answers that do not refer directly to the picture narrative are not acceptable – however reasonable and plausible.

An example of two poor responses to an inference question:

> Question: Are the <u>people</u> in the picture <u>making clothes</u> for a <u>giant</u>? How do you know that?
>
> Answer 1: Yes.
>
> Answer 2: Yes, because they have drawn a picture of him.

Comment

The first response does not fully answer the question because the second part of the question asks them to give evidence that shows how they know the answer is 'yes'.

The second response is incorrect because the reader has not considered the question closely enough. They have not accurately identified the clues in the question – *people, making clothes, giant* – and linked them to the inferred clues in the picture narrative – *little people, measuring and sewing material, clothes pattern, giant feet* – to provide an answer that is supported by clear evidence.

In addition, it is helpful for readers to know that if they use part of the question to answer with, it will guide their answers and help to keep them on the right track.

> Correct answer: *Yes, the **people** in the picture are **making clothes for a giant**. I know this* because *there is a pair of **giant feet** in the picture and next to them much **smaller** people are **cutting** and **sewing large rolls of material** from a **clothes pattern** designed for a **very large man**.*

Evaluation – personal meaning. What you think characters may be feeling, doing or thinking from clues within the narrative and your own experience of life. Expressing an opinion based on information given.

Evaluation questions vary considerably according to the reader's own experience and prior knowledge. However, whatever their response, it must relate to the information given in the picture to be acceptable.

An example of two poor responses to an evaluation question:

> Question: *Do you think* some of the *characters* are *finding their task difficult*? *Why* do you say that?
>
> Answer 1: Yes.
>
> Answer 2: No, because I think the design they are using looks easy to understand.

Comment

The first answer is incomplete because the person has not given a reason for their answer. The second response is inappropriate. The reader has not focused on all the key words in the question. Instead they have based their answer too much on personal opinion that is not supported by evidence from the picture. Although the reader has considered whether the 'task' is 'difficult', they have not linked this to the other key clue in the question that refers to the 'characters' in the picture. Consequently, they have not looked for facial expressions and body language in the picture that suggest how the characters might be feeling or thinking about 'their task'.

> Appropriate answer: *Yes, I think some of the characters are finding their task difficult because **they are puzzling** over the clothes design and **looking unsure** about it.*

Clarification – understanding the meaning of vocabulary or a concept within the context of picture narrative. Defining the meaning of a word or concept from evidence available in a picture.

Readers of 'Snapshot' are asked to infer and define the meaning for words or ideas in the images by making links with clues in the picture narrative.

An example of a poor response to a clarification question:

Question: There is a small man in the picture using a _megaphone_. Explain _what_ he is using this _device_ for.

Answer: He is using a megaphone because he is making a long distance phone call.

Comment

The reader has answered the question incorrectly because although he has used prior knowledge to try to guess the meaning of the word, he has not referred to clues in the picture that suggest *what the device is* and *what it is being used for*. His answer does not make sense in the context of the picture.

Correct answer: *The small man in the picture is using a megaphone to make his* **tiny voice** *louder so the tailors who are measuring the giant* **high above** *him* **can hear what he is saying**.

Assessing levels – marking

Each comprehension level is a based on marks out of 20 that are represented as a percentage score at the end of the assessment, for example 2/20 = 10%; 12/20 – 60% and so on. The marks range from 1–3 points according to the question type. The marks for question types can be correlated with the QCA SATs marking system and are as follows:

- Literal: 1 point
- Inference: 2 points
- Prediction: 2 points
- Clarification: 2 points
- Evaluation: 3 points

The reader's total score represents a snapshot of their ability to gather information, summarise, predict, clarify and finally ask and answer literal, inferential and evaluative questions from pictures and titles. Ability within each level is measured to establish whether the reader or team need to drop down a level to help them to develop their comprehension skills further; need to remain at the same level to receive further instructional support; or are accomplished enough to move on to challenges on the next level. This can be used as evidence for a periodic assessment of the children's comprehension skills.

Comprehension ability within level

Easy/secure	score 70–100%	(move to next level)
Instructional/partial	score 40–65%	(remain at this level)
Hard/insecure	score 0–35%	(move down a level)

Notes